Happy & Glorious

A Royal Celebration

Fellowship & Fairydust

2023

CONTENTS

King Charles II by Godfrey
Kneller, 1685/1865

EDITOR'S NOTE

"Monarchy can easily be 'debunked,' but watch the faces, mark well the debunkers. These are the men whose taproot in Eden has been cut: whom no rumour of the polyphony, the dance, can reach - men to whom pebbles laid in a row are more beautiful than an arch."

\- C. S. Lewis

Monarchy in the modern world is sometimes dismissed as an anachronism, a relic of feudal times, antithetical to the spirit of meritocracy and leveling of hierarchies that marks out modern progress. And yet, some of the countries that score highest on metrics of democracy, accountability, personal freedom, equality under the law and equality of income, are in fact monarchies-not just the United Kingdom's world-famous Royal Family referred to affectionately as 'The Firm', but also the lesser-known royal families of Spain, Norway, Sweden, Denmark, the Netherlands, Belgium, and Japan. All these states score immensely well on global metrics of human development, and all have proved determined to maintain their royal families despite the pressures of modernity.

It would seem that monarchy is not in practice a barrier to the liberation of the human spirit, and that some countries have found a way that it can *enhance* it-providing a focal point for national unity and a lodestar for the national conscience, above the petty partisan concerns of elected presidents and politicians with one eye on their re-election. Indeed, it seems republics are afflicted with many of the same cons of national life experienced under monarchies, but also bereft of the benefits. Perhaps it is wrong-headed to presume republics have embraced, by default, the singular 'mature' form of government, or indeed to romanticize them as the best, or even only, system under which freedom can flourish.

And what of 'The Firm', which will soon crown a new King to reign over not only Britain but Canada, Australia, New Zealand, and numerous other Commonwealth Realms with an ancestral link to the United Kingdom? All evidence suggests that, despite recent challenges, it remains in rude health. Although the memory of the late Queen-Britain's 'national grandmother'-endure, both at home and abroad, Britons have in large part embraced King Charles III as a worthy successor, with polls revealing overwhelming public confidence in his suitability for the job, and almost unanimous approval for his first King's Speech to the nation. Moreover, the King is a born innovator, well-placed to ensure the monarchy remains relevant and responds to the concerns of a changing society. In trying times for Britain and for the world, the coronation is generally being greeted as a moment for optimism and hope, in which a new chapter of history is personified in a visible and tangible way.

How does a monarchy-an institution that, its detractors would tell us, is founded on feudal principles of brutality and oppression of the powerless by the powerful-command such widespread respect, and manage to unite such large swathes of a nation where elected and supposedly more 'representative' leaders so often fail? Perhaps it is because most monarchs in developed countries-whose involvement in politics is largely symbolic-stand above the fray as a sort of personification of the nation itself, a figure to whom one can turn for confidence in an unstable world. When the late Queen Elizabeth II asked Britons to come together in solidarity during the Covid pandemic and encouraged them to believe that 'we will meet again' when the crisis had passed, the British people believed her.

But more than that, the imagery and symbolism of monarchy plays into centuries of tradition and a rich mythic and poetic background that creates the sense of an enduring connection between past and present. It is unhealthy to cut the present off from its roots in the hopes of creating an unrealistic utopia of the future. The unbroken line of continuity that modern monarchs represent binds together various strands of shared heritage, reminding us not to idolize the transient threads of the present and to cast our eyes to something more spiritually enriching and purposeful than a merely consumer-based society.

Stories of kings and queens, from our first childhood experiences of fairy stories to our explorations of real and complex historical events, have the power to stir the imagination and to awaken deep, hidden, and potent currents in the human soul. In many ways, monarchs are archetypes writ large of what each of us can be in our own particular role in life. Ritual and symbolism are not as empty as many people, leaning towards soulless materialism, might insist. We are, by nature, spiritual beings seeking belonging; the magic of monarchy instinctively and inescapably appeals to something beyond explanation, especially in the modern world which is mystically impoverished.

For the great religious traditions, tales of kingship–whether righteous or tyrannical–also have resonance and weight. King Charles III's decision not to televise the moment of his coronation when he is anointed with holy oil can be seen as a profound acknowledgement of the reality of the promise he is making, both to himself and, according to his sincere belief, to God, that–to quote his mother–his 'whole life, whether it be long or short, shall be devoted to your service.'

In this, we might see what C.S. Lewis called the 'taproot in Eden', where Adam, the archetypal and primordial first Man, might be seen being called out from all other creatures as a type of king among creation. This intense personalism of 'I' and 'Thou' between God and Man is expressed uniquely in this continuation of consecration. In light of Christian tradition, it might even be seen as an imperfect reflection of the Incarnation, when the divine and human are brought together the person of Christ the King.

Here at *Fellowship & Fairydust*, we have put together an anthology to explore that mythopoetic hinterland that makes monarchy continue to resonate in the minds of those alive today. It is an honour for us to unveil this multifaceted issue in commemoration both of the passing of Queen Elizabeth II and the accession of Charles III, by the Grace of God, of the United Kingdom of Great Britain and Northern Ireland and of his other Realms and Territories Overseas King, Defender of the Faith.

Among our diverse featured pieces, we have a story about a chance meeting with King George III at a garden party; a reflection on the continued importance of the legacy of King Charles I and the mythos of martyrdom; a story following Bonnie Prince Charlie on his flight through the Highlands and islands of Scotland; a memoir about a Protestant Orangeman's pilgrimage in the footsteps of William III; a story about King Henry V at his father's funeral, struggling to find God's will through his own calling to lead; an article about the prospection cause for canonization of the Catholic exile King James II; and a story about King Henry VIII's tragic friendship with Sir Thomas More.

In addition to these and many more pieces on royals from history, legend, and literature, there are various articles commenting on the passing of the mantle from the late Queen Elizabeth II to her son King Charles III, and the religious and historical significance of the ceremonies surrounding this transfer of symbolic–and therefore quite real–power. We hope that, as the world watches the coronation unfold, this anthology will prove an educational and enjoyable survey of the illustrious event and the many facets of monarchy, past and present.

God save the King!

Best wishes and every blessing,

Avellina Balestri

Editor-in-Chief

Christian Owen

Secretary

*Portrait of George III of the United
Kingdom in parliamentary robes*
by Thomas Gainsborough, 1785

A ROYAL MEETING

Avellina Balestri

Author's Note: The following is an excerpt from the duology in progress, "All Ye Who Pass By", which follows the experiences of Edmund Southworth (alias Ned), a young man from an English Catholic Recusant family who finds himself drawn into the turbulence of the American Revolution.

Several days later, Edmund found himself whisked off to an elaborate garden party where Colonel Burgoyne mixed and mingled amiably with London elites of every stripe. Ned, for his part, stayed out of the way as much as possible, awkwardly hovering over a punch bowl, but drinking very little. For all his blue blood, he was a country mouse among country mice, and felt more at home at a harvest dance than at a lavish gala. Besides, any gathering with too many people milling about tended to make him nervous.

Suddenly there was a fanfare of horns, and the assembly grew hushed.

Burgoyne leaned over and whispered in Edmund's ear, "It's the King. Stand up straight."

Ned dropped his ladle of punch with a splash and clank. "You-you didn't tell me that—"

"Didn't I? Oh well. Surprise!"

Edmund had the sudden desire to throw himself under the table and remain hidden until the royal visitation was over. Part of this was because he realized to his dismay that he had just spilled punch on his white ruffled shirt, making it look as if he had been stabbed in an ill-fated fencing lesson, and that his blood ran an insipid pink shade; the other part was simply the knee-jerk reaction of a recusant.

Catholics might well sing about "Great George, our King" to soothe the trepidation of their Protestant neighbors, but few would be entirely comfortable with him showing up in the flesh to scrutinize them. They were, after all, ostracized by virtue of their continued refusal to acknowledge him as governor of the Church in England. What kept them firm in their conviction was the sacraments, and those sacraments were brought to the faithful by priests, forbidden to minister in England. The harboring of those self-same priests made the faithful ever-so-slightly akin to outlaws, and Ned was far from exempt on this account. But too late now, too late, now...

In the course of all that worrying, the King had already made his grand entrance, moved along through the garden party, and planted himself like a statue in front of them. Ned imitated Burgoyne in bowing, but continued to keep his eyes down, which made him even more fixated upon his stained shirt. He felt sure his face was turning as pink as the punch.

He looked up slightly as the King and Burgoyne exchanged courtesies. Burgoyne, as usual, was taking the opportunity to gush and grandstand, but Ned was in no frame of mind to process his monologue, beyond something to do with His Majesty's inestimable virtues, and Burgoyne's inestimable talents, and the troublemakers among the colonials needing to be put in their place. Ned found himself noticing that the King's clothes were formal but not showy, the kind any dignified country gentlemen would wear, as opposed to Burgoyne's ostentatious fare. And on his jacket was pinned a very pretty button.

After that, Ned vaguely recalled the King asking him a direct question, which his terrified state of mind translated as "Who are you?" He found himself numbly replying, "Yes, sire," followed by something-something "pretty button," and was absolutely horrified by his own voice sounding so childish. He felt Burgoyne nudge him in the ribs, adding to his mortification.

The King was looking at Edmund full in the face now, his large blue eyes slightly perplexed.

"Your button, sire... it's very fine... yes, very fine indeed..."

He was going to die. He was sure of it now.

"Indeed," concurred the King in perfect monotone. "It is for our patronage of The Handel Society."

"Oh... wonderful, I mean... well done," Ned replied, desperately trying to find some conversational footing. "I-I have always admired him, s-s-sire."

Joy to the world. He was stuttering now. Someone needed to just take him out back and put him out of his misery.

But to his surprise, he saw a slight smile play on the King's mouth. It was not unkind.

"As you may know, our grandfather was the first to stand for the Hallelujah at the performance of Handel's Messiah in London," he stated.

"Yes, sire," Ned replied, "because the power of the piece moved him."

The King leaned forward slightly, and said in a quieter voice, "It was not without precedent for our grandfather to drift into slumber during performances. When he was subsequently roused, momentary confusion, accompanied by eagerness to suitably respond to what could have been the royal anthem, might naturally follow..."

"Ahhh," Ned exhaled."

"We are not, of course, saying this is in fact how it happened," the King stated gingerly. "We honor the tradition our grandfather set by standing to this day, and we are wide awake."

"Me too," Ned blurted. "I mean...I

Ned found himself noticing that the King's clothes were formal but not showy, the kind any dignified country gentlemen would wear, as opposed to Burgoyne's ostentatious fare.

stand, and we all stand, because You're Majesty stands, and I think it's altogether right we all do so."

"We recall first listening to it, and standing, when we were yet a prince," the King reflected. "We afterwards met the composer backstage. We have not forgotten that, nor shall we. We have purchased his harpsichord. We play it, even."

"That's marvelous, sire," Ned responded cheerfully, genuinely pleased to hear the instrument was still in use.

"We hope the original owner doesn't mind too terribly, wherever he is," the King remarked. "His genius was matched by a temper. Nearly ran a man through for touching the instrument."

"If there's anyone he wouldn't mind having it, and playing it, surely it would be you," Edmund assured him. "You-you wear his button, after all…"

The King chuckled. "Do you play, hmm?"

"My sister does, though I am no good," Ned admitted. "I-I do drop everything and listen, though, whenever goodly music is being played. It's like… like a prayer, like everything we could feel… joy and sorrow and glory, and the brevity of here, and the eyes eternity of there…" He caught himself rambling, and thought of some way to finish. "It is all life, in a twinkling. I believe it is Handel said…he saw the face of God."

"Yes," the King said softly. "That is Handel." He turned to Burgoyne, who seemed to have gone into a blank stare, no longer being the center of attention. "This one… he's not the same as the one who was here last time, is he?"

"No, Your Majesty," Burgoyne replied, relocating himself. "I'm afraid not. He's not as accustomed to garden parties…"

"Afraid?" The king's eyes glimmered with irony. "No need, sir, no need. At least this one is sober, with brightness in his eyes. The garden parties have not managed to dull them yet, what?"

Edmund chuckled a little. Then the King turned back to him, took off his button, and extended it to him. "Become a member of the Society."

Edmund felt a flush of mixed emotions. "I would, sire, truly… but it costs… quite a bit, doesn't it? That is to say, I am not very—"

"We are making a gift of membership to you, with this," the King clarified.

Ned blinked. "Are you… are you sure you want me to take it? It's a very fine button…"

"We have a box," the King retorted with a shrug.

"Oh… well, in that case…" He took the King's button. "Thank you very kindly."

The King gestured at a specific point on Ned's shirt where the punch had stained particularly badly. "If you affix it *there*, it might cover *that*."

Ned felt his face burning, but did as he was instructed.

The King nodded in satisfaction and said, "We wish you success in your military career, and continued good health wherever duty takes you."

"Thank you, Your Maj-"

"Oh, he's not a recruit, sire," Burgoyne chortled, with a flippant gesture of his hand. "Faith, he cannot be, I fear! He is a Papist! Lancashire recusant family, fine father, lent me some coin when I was hard-pressed, diamond necklace for a young lady, had to pawn it, you understand, passed on, poor soul, and here is his lad, under my wing…"

Ned felt quite sure he was going to have to dive under the table now.

The King stared at Burgoyne as if the man was slightly touched, then glanced over to Ned, as if to ask whether or not this was a hostage crisis that required intervention. At last, he turned back to Burgoyne.

"When next you see your lady wife, pray tell her we send her every felicitation, along with our Queen," the King said evenly, as if to put Burgoyne in his place, and Ned, struck by the humor of the situation, and Burgoyne's chastened expression, could not prevent himself from smiling momentarily. Then the King turned back to Ned, causing his smile to fade. "A recusant, are you?"

"Yes, Your Majesty," Edmund confirmed, butterflies in his stomach.

"Have you made any renovations to your house of late?"

"No, sire," Ned answered cautiously, guessing the query might well refer to priest holes and secret chapels. "We have everything we need already."

"We see," the King said, a dubious glint in his eyes. "It is good to take care in such matters. Too many alterations risk unsettling their foundation, after all."

"We are very keen to keep our foundation solid, Your Majesty."

"And in terms of your daily bread," the King continued, "what is your source of sustenance up there?"

Edmund found himself saying, perhaps unwisely, "Very little to speak of, Your Majesty, save for the sacrifice of Christ."

Any recusant would have known the double meaning, would have known that he meant the sacrifice of the Holy Mass which they risked so much to attend.

But the King seemed unaware of it, or at least chose to act as if he was unaware of it. In fact, he seemed to approve of Ned's choice of answer, and replied simply, "That too is my dependency."

And Edmund saw in that moment George the Third not only as his sovereign, but as a sinner, like himself, saved by grace. And as the King departed, Ned felt no separation between them.

LONG MAY SHE REIGN: THE LIFE OF QUEEN ELIZABETH II

Michael Goth

When Queen Elizabeth II died on September 8, 2022, at age 96, she had been Queen of England for 70 years, longer than any other British monarch. Three months before her death, she had celebrated a seven-decade reign with her Platinum Jubilee.

Elizabeth Alexandra Mary Windsor was born on April 21, 1926, the first child of the Duke and Duchess of York, in Mayfair, London. Her sister, Margaret, followed on August 9, 1930. The sisters would remain close their entire lives.

Elizabeth had a relatively normal childhood, considering she was a member of the royal family. She was fond of horses and dogs and had 30 total corgis during her life. Elizabeth and Margaret also trained ponies. The princesses received an at-home education in history, language, literature and music under the guidance of their mother and governess, Marion Crawford.

In 1950, against the wishes of the royal family, Crawford published a book, The Little Princesses, about her work with Elizabeth and Margaret. In the 2001 book Royal: Her Majesty Queen Elizabeth II, author Robert Lacey wrote about an encounter at Balmoral Castle between Winston Churchill and the princess when Elizabeth was only two years old, in which the prime minister said, "She has an air of authority and reflectiveness astonishing in an infant." A queen in the making.

Elizabeth had never expected to become an heir to the throne, as her uncle Edward was first in line as successor, then her father. Edward III became king in January 1936 upon the death of Elizabeth's grandfather, George V. George VI became the King of England on December 11, 1936, after Edward gave up the throne and married divorced American socialite Wallis Simpson.

On September 3, 1939, Britain declared war on Nazi Germany. Europe was at war. To keep the princesses safe, Lord Hailsham recommended

Photo: *Portrait of Elizabeth II* by Donald McKague, 1958

that Elizabeth and Margaret be taken to Canada, while England was being bombed by the Nazis. The Duchess of York turned down the suggestion, saying, "The children will not go without me. I won't leave without the King, And the King will never leave." Fourteen-year-old Elizabeth gave her first radio broadcast for the BBC's Children's Hour in October 1940 with a message for the young people who had been evacuated from their homes in the wake of the Blitz, "My sister, Margaret Rose, and I feel so much for you as we know from experience what it means to be away from those we love most of all."

In 1944, at age 18, Elizabeth joined the wartime women's unit the Auxiliary Territorial Serve where she worked as a truck driver and mechanic. In May of the following year, she joined the celebration in Victory in Europe Day following Germany's surrender, which she said was among "the most memorable nights of my life."

On July 9, 1947, 21-year-old Elizabeth announced her engagement to the 26-year-old Prince Philip of Greece and Denmark. They were married four months later at Westminster Abbey.

Philip Mountbatten was born on June 10, 1921. After finishing his education in France, Germany and the United Kingdom, the young prince joined the Royal Navy in 1939, serving in the British Mediterranean and the Pacific fleets during the Second World War. Philip met Elizabeth in 1934 and again in 1937, they later exchanged frequent correspondence. Elizabeth and Philip were secretly engaged in 1946. Once married, King George made Philip the Duke of Edinburgh.

Elizabeth and Philip were married until his death on April 9, 2021, having four children: Charles in 1948, Anne in 1950, Andrew in 1960, and Edward in 1964.

Elizabeth and Philip were on tour in Kenya when George VI died on February 6, 1952. Elizabeth was still asleep, and Philip had to wake her to tell her of her father's death. Elizabeth assumed her role as Queen Elizabeth II.

Along with her role as queen, Elizabeth was also the Supreme Governor and Defender of the Church of England. Several recent books, including The Faith of Queen Elizabeth by Dudley Delffs, have explored Elizabeth's religious beliefs.

Delffs—a novelist, poet, and biographer who has written about the faith of everyone from Elizabeth to Dolly Parton—writes about how growing up, King George VI and the Queen Mother made sure Elizabeth and Margaret attended weekly Mass and read from their King James Bibles, having them memorize favorite pieces of scripture from Psalms. Delffs believes that the Queen's inner kindness was also a result of her religious beliefs.

England has long enjoyed a special bond with the United States, which extended to Queen Elizabeth's relationship with many American presidents. She met Harry Truman in October of 1951 in Washington, D.C., before she was queen, and would meet with all the U.S. presidents with the exception of Lyndon B. Johnson. Elizabeth had tea with President Joe Biden and First lady Jill Biden in Windsor on June 13, 2021, a little more than a year before her death. In 1982, Ronald Reagan became the first U.S. President to spend the night in Windsor.

George W. Bush and Donald Trump's visits with the Queen were not met with open arms from the English people. When Bush visited London in November 2003, 100,000 of the Queen's subjects took to the street to protest the Iraq War, which was even more unpopular in England than it was in America—where it was very controversial. When Trump met the Queen in Windsor in July 2018, protestors took to the streets to convey their disapproval of the American president's overall crude behavior, especially his negative attitude toward LGBTQ and human issues.

Like all families Elizabeth's had its share of problems. However, when one is a member of the royal family, personal issues often become a public drama. Prince Charles's 1981 wedding to Diana Spencer was seen as almost a fairy tale marriage, but the couple separated in 1994, with Diana telling the press that she and her husband had both been unfaithful. Charles and Diana were officially divorced in 1996, with the former Lady Diana dying in an auto accident a year later, leaving behind her two children with Charles—William and Harry.

Prince Andrew married Sarah Ferguson in 1986 and divorced a decade later having had two daughters—Beatrice and Eugenie. In 2014, Virginia Giuffree, a campaigner who created the Victim's Refuse Silence, and was one of many young women who accused Jeffrey Epstein of trafficking her in his sex ring, claimed that Andrew had sexually assaulted her at age 17. Though the prince claimed innocence and a lawsuit was settled out of court in 2022, Andrew stepped down from all public roles.

Queen Elizabeth continued to be a sign of hope for her subjects into the twenty-first century. As A.N. Wilson wrote in Time magazine for their special issue on the life of the Queen, when 22 people were killed in Manchester in 2017, when a suicide bomber set off an explosive at an Ariana Grande concert, Elizabeth visited the injured children at Royal Manchester's Children's Hospital and provided comforting words in the aftermath of the attack in that year's annual Christmas message.

Elizabeth also provided comfort to the English people during the COVID-19 Pandemic. She herself went into COVID lockdown at Windsor castle.

Following COVID restrictions, the Queen sat alone at the funeral of her husband of over 70 years when King Philip died on April 9, 2021. In her Christmas broadcast eight months later, she spoke of the love she had for her "beloved Philip."

On September 8, 2022, Elizabeth died at age 96 with her family at her side. She was mourned by the entire world.

Long may she reign.

MY CROWN I GAVE UP FOR YOU

G. Connor Salter

You know that it could have been you there on the throne.

Merlin sighed and looked at the window. Halfway through the coronation, he had known something infernal had entered the courtyard.

The proceedings had begun well. The Archbishop had asked Merlin to give a summary—the old king's death, Merlin placing Arthur in Sir Ector's care, the sword in the stone which only Arthur could remove—allegedly because some of the lower-ranking knights present had been only children when Uther Pendragon passed. Merlin suspected the Archbishop felt a ceremony wasn't a proper one unless it took all day. He had reached the part about Kay trying to take credit for removing the sword from the stone when he felt the hairs on his neck and shoulders rise. Arthur looked concerned as Merlin paused. Merlin kept talking and no one else seemed to notice.

The presence made itself clearer as the ceremony continued. When the Archbishop told his servants to bring out the crown, Merlin could hear a sharp wind rattling a tree near the chapel wall. When the servants brought out the oak chest, one of the servants kept his eyes on Merlin as the other opened it. The wind picked up. One of the tree's branches clattered against a stained-glass window. The servant kept staring at Merlin as his partner handed him the crown. A larger branch smacked against the window. The servant fumbled, the crown falling from his hands. Merlin crouched and caught it before it struck the floor.

The presence was impossible to ignore now. His shoulders—large shoulders, the monks said they were large because he was born to wear wings—sweated. The crown felt warm. Far warmer than it should have felt after decades in a cellar. The branch rattled a constant beat against the window.

Merlin stood and handed the crown to the servant. The servant snatched it and passed it to the Archbishop. The Archbishop hissed for the servant to leave, then turned to place it on Arthur's head. As the servant went to a side door, he looked at Merlin

Artwork: *King Arthur* by Charles Ernest Butler, 1903

again and made the sign of the cross. Merlin wasn't surprised. What surprised him was that the servant didn't whisper anything as he left. He was used to people whispering when he passed.

Demon spawn. Child of hell. Antichrist. Madman of the woods. Even the druids fear him.

Once the crown was on Arthur's head, the branches stopped rattling the window. The ceremony ended with Arthur on his throne, promising to do right by all God's laws, then giving out knighthoods and listening to pleas for aid. The Archbishop had said a few words about the appropriateness of crowning a new king at Pentecost, when the church was born anew, and then signaled for the feast to start. Sir Ector had made sure Merlin had a prominent place at a corner table near Arthur. Merlin hadn't commented on the fact it was across the hall from the Archbishop and church representatives. It also happened to be directly across the hall from the window.

While others chatted and ate, Merlin sipped his wine and examined the window. It depicted the Holy Mother meeting the angel Gabriel. The tree behind it didn't move. It looked a little too still.

That was when he heard the voice.

That could have been you on that throne.

Merlin picked up his goblet and signaled a page for more wine. Once he had it, Merlin stood. Arthur's gaze met him as he rose. Merlin smiled, patted his stomach, and cocked his head to the side door. Arthur grinned and nodded. Kay—Sir Kay now—leaned toward Arthur's ear. The two foster brothers laughed, and neither noticed when Merlin left the hall.

The courtyard was empty when Merlin entered it. Merlin approached the tree. His sweat had covered his inner garment, making it stick to his back. As he neared the tree, a shadow across its largest branch took a new shape. It became a winged man, with hunched shoulders and a broad back.

"Lucien," Merlin said. "It has been some time since you last visited me."

The shadow cocked his head.

"You were so close," the shadow said. "What did you think of that servant boy's face when he looked at you? Did it seem proper for him to treat a son of a prince of Hell so poorly? Did you think about turning him into a mouse and crushing him?"

"He's a foolish boy," Merlin answered. "One day someone will explain to him that once baptized means once sanctified."

The shadow reached for a thin branch above. It snapped the branch off. It turned the branch over in its hands, stripping away the leaves.

"There was so much that went into making you possible," the shadow said. "I still remember my master's words. 'Our abode may be harrowed, but our battle continues. We will make a man of our own image, schooled in vengeance and vigor. The prophets may have deceived us, but our prophet will return it tenfold.' It was our greatest effort. The Infernal Council caroused for a month after your conception."

Merlin pulled back his cloak and reached for his shoulder. His hand separated the inner garment from his skin, and he rubbed his shoulder. He had worn his thinnest hairshirt to avoid damaging the nice clothes Arthur had given him for the feast. It still chafed.

Merlin withdrew his hand and held up a piece of the hairshirt. "Perhaps the prophet part suits me," he said.

The shadow held the branch like a pan flute. "I'm sure your mother was pleased that you wear it," it said. "Still, who can say what she wanted? I remember your father's words. 'I can place seed in a woman, and I know a woman I can corrupt. By the time I have had my way, she will not know herself.'"

Merlin clenched his goblet. A blue

flame rose over the wine. He raised the goblet.

The shadow stopped playing with the branch. "Go on. You're no lackey to a bastard English boy. Do you truly think an aborted antichrist can bring forth a savior? Be what you know you are."

Merlin stared at the blue fire. The wine steamed. The goblet radiated heat. It would blister his fingers in a few moments.

He lowered the goblet. The blue fire faded. He looked back at the shadow.

"I know what I am," Merlin said. "I know I am the bastard son of Hell's princeling. I know I was born to un-make the Lord's work. I know I seem a fool to you. But I will not play your games."

The shadow threw the branch. It ignited in mid-flight. Merlin caught it before it struck the window. When his gaze returned to the tree, the shadow was gone.

Merlin raised the cup and drank the hot wine. The sun had set. He turned and went back to his king's coronation feast.

This story is expanded from "The Light Bringer," a 150-word short story that appeared in the audio collection Tapes from the Crawlspace. *Original story copyright 2020 by Gabriel Connor Salter.*

The story of Merlin's conception appears in a twelfth- or thirteenth-century poem written by Robert de Boron. The quotations from the demons in Hell are original dialogue, written as a loose paraphrase of the poem's demon quotations (lines 36-42, 47-48 in "The Birth of Merlin," as published in the 1998 translation of Prose Merlin *edited by John Conlee, published by Medieval Institute Publications). I also consulted Nigel Bryant's translation of the poem, included in* Merlin and the Grail *(D.S. Brewer, 2005, Kindle edition). Both translations are copyrighted, and no infringement is made or intended.*

"REMEMBER": ON THE CULTUS OF CHARLES I

Sean Earner

Piety is an all-serving, all-mastering virtue by which to inhabit both the modern and the postmodern present alike. Its homely humility bears within itself a hidden power by which all the dryness, doubt, and darkness are made into the very conditions of its victory. We often hear the laments, or celebrations, of the rise of irreligion and attacks on faith by the forces of secularism. But what is often forgotten in such debates is that the present epoch is one that invites and unprecedentedly enables the virtue of devotion, for those who have eyes to see, ears to hear, and voices to lift in praise.

"Attention, taken to its highest degree, is the same thing as prayer," said the philosopher Simone Weil. And the opportunity to give attention is now more present than ever. One can read, listen, watch, and engage with far more than was possible before and multiply one's experience by connection with others who wish to provide their testimony to the mystery they have sensed in the contemporary wasteland.

Many abuse this historical chance to exhaust their souls in excessive fandoms, pseudo-relationships with podcasters, shallow commercial monomanias, and other objects of sad passions. But that should not make us cynical about the potential for good that we have here and now. Technology and the pious disposition towards the world are not intrinsically opposites, contrary to both certain secularists and certain traditionalists, but can be and in fact in many cases are, partners towards a more flourishing human condition that brings together all the paradigms of human experience in a whole that is both rich in surface beauty and hidden depths as it moves with stately speed together towards a divine climax that we can only dimly imagine. In this brave divided world, still so old and so new at the same time, many are the icons to revere, many the rites in which to join the festive throng, many the sacred orders in which to receive initiation.

King Charles I, who was executed by the Parliamentarians at the conclu-

Artwork: *Portrait of King Charles I* by Anthony van Dyck, c. 1635

sion of the English Civil War, yet raised to victory as a martyred saint in Anglicanism, is an unlikely occasion for devotion by an Irish-American Catholic. And in previous historical moments, it would never have happened. Yet the collapse of temporal and spatial boundaries that has accompanied the cyber present leads to unlikely meetings. I have always respected the beheaded monarch in a relatively cool state of mind. But, finding on social media a link to a High Mass in honor of his feast day January 30, I was enthralled by the ritual sounds and music of the liturgy as I drove home from work. More deeply though, I was moved as never before by the regal but vulnerable person at the center of this both mournful and triumphant Christian festival. When I got home, I looked up online a description of his end, fastening especially to the line said to his servant that "this is my second marriage day... for before night I hope to be espoused to my blessed Jesus." Rich and deep associations with the writings of the saints and mystics—especially those of Carmel, to which I am bound as a secular member—were stirred.

I found an audiobook biography, Charles I: An Abbreviated Life by Mark Kishlansky, and listened to it, fascinated by someone who was both clearly very human yet also capable of striving for holiness and for the uncreated Good despite the sadness and perils of the world. In the midst of this I decided to link up and join the Society of King Charles the Martyr, making an offering to his memory and in hope of his intercession from among the crowd of witnesses that have been gathered from every age, place, and nation. In the course of 24 hours, the last word of Charles, "Remember," had reached personal fulfillment in my own mind and heart. The relay of the centuries had reached its destination, in the seemingly unlikely hyper-mediated experience of the virtual.

Not only did the technological condition enable this meeting of souls but it added a new force to the experience. Piety when truly embraced by an emancipated modern subject has an intensified charm and enticement. That one embraces God and his saints is all the more worthy when the conditions on the surface are so unfavorable. It becomes a calling that we truly and undeniably chose. Religious liberty thus adds to the merit of fidelity.

The writer Jorge Luis Borges once wrote a short story, "Pierre Menard, Author of the *Quixote*." Borges considers Menard's fragmentary *Quixote* (which is line-for-line identical to the original) to be much richer in allusion than Miguel de Cervantes' "original" work. Borges' analysis describes Menard's efforts to go beyond a mere "translation" of *Don Quixote* by immersing himself comprehensively in the work as to be able to actually remake it, line for line. Menard's text must be considered in light of world events since 1602. Borges feels that any man who chooses to repeat that novel in modern times in its entirety has given it a new meaning that cannot be reduced to its predecessor.

This paradoxical line can be invoked in the case of contemporary faith. That we choose to offer up prayers for God in the present epoch means we have added a unique note to the chorus of creation. To adore the Eucharist, to pray at the office, to wear on one's person the mark of Christ and the saints, has an added beauty in an age in which God and the gods have left a space of emptiness and silence. We prove through prayers and deeds that the divine has not fled its post cowardly but has rather given us a testing ground and preparatory room to prove ourselves as true sons. Our modern freedom can, and is, gravely abused by some. But to many others is a way of participating in the mystery of

Golgotha, and that of the empty tomb.

The Reformation and the Counter-Reformation are in many respects unresolved battles and this obviously affects how one is to view devotion to the Royal Martyr. There are interesting arguments to be made that the cultus of Charles can be someday considered a valid one from within the Catholic communion, taking up a place in the truly universal public worship of Christians everywhere. One can pray and work for such a victory of ecumenism, all the more beautiful, fitting, and necessary because it would be between Christians who take Catholicity seriously as the mark and heritage of the faith. The Church has already made great efforts to reconcile with the Eastern Orthodox that were estranged by schism. Through the Ordinariate, we have begun to take serious steps to reconcile the Anglican patrimony with the Universal Body of Christ. To accept and promote the cultus of Charles I would be a striking and gallant way of approaching ever greater and more perfect union. There is no more sure and more admirable way of loving our erstwhile enemies than to acknowledge that their dead are not lacking in worth and heroism.

For now, in my status as a private layman of Rome, I will pray for him as a fellow sinner and, if he is indeed among the elect, hope for his prayers in turn. May his beatitude, whether already realized, or to come, be preserved and magnified in the flickering votive candle of my soul.

What specifically inspires admiration in the person of Charles? To put it simply, it is his qualities as a good Christian layman, his fidelity to his role as king, and his imitation of Christ as a suffering servant.

As a private man, Charles I was marked by a sense of honor, an instinct for justice, and above all a spirit of clemency. As he would repeat to his confidantes, he believed that he would prefer to be deceived than to distrust. He did not have the private vices of meanness of spirit and paranoia that are the marks of a man without internal integrity in the exercise of power.

Further, like Emperor Charles I of Austria, with whom our English monarch shared a name and so much more, he was a loving husband to his wife and father to his children, with an exalted Christian sense of both roles. Significantly, he never took a mistress even though it was a common practice of crowned heads of state at the time. Despite the troubled beginnings of his marriage, he grew to treat his spouse as a true partner in divine union.

Finally, and most importantly, he was devoted to the Virgin Mary, the saints, the relics of the same, and the Blessed Sacrament, much to the consternation of his Protestant subjects and the joys of those who took the Catholic identity of the British church seriously. He was a true heir to the Renaissance and the Baroque, lover of the arts and humanist learning. But he did not cease to carry forward the banner of the age of faith. His mind and imagination remained formed by the ancient and medieval rhythms of divine worship and praise, preserving it in the midst of an epicenter of the Reformation.

One can debate indefinitely the wisdom of this or that detail of Charles' reign, the forced vs unforced nature of his errors which led to the unprecedented execution of an English monarch. If political success is the ultimate criterion, then Charles was a resounding failure. But what cannot be denied is that Charles was faithful to the royal office despite many adversaries and setbacks, embracing the aura of kingship and playing out that role of life to the end. In him was fulfilled the mystery of the sovereign as a sacramental image of divine rule, a special image of mankind as the Vicegerent of creation. This, paradoxically, made him even more determined to be a servant to the People, and to be their martyr. His awareness of the sacred origin of his legitimacy led him not to take for granted his power over others. It was a true grace, and thus a true gift that, to use his own words, enabled the enjoyment of the subjects under the canopy of the radically distinct sovereign.

But what above all makes Charles such a powerful image of sanctity was his end. He went to the scaffold with courage, grace, and flair, praying for mercy towards those who had condemned him and presenting eloquently the case for his cause, conscious of living out a drama that was both religious, political, and uniquely personal. An earthly king, through defeat and disgrace, lived out the paradox of the crowned victim. His imitation of Christ reached its fulfillment in the conclusion of his life, giving away the corruptible that he had been blessed so abundantly with to possess the incorruptible. It is as hard for a camel to pass through the eye of a needle as for a rich man to gain heaven. But Charles Stuart suggested that this hard saying does not make the saving light unavailable even for those most blessed by birth in the favors of the world.

Charles impresses upon the mind an image of sanctity that fascinates and inspires with its goodness from his mundane private existence to his royal office to his glorious exit after the humiliation of defeat. He lived the life of a good ordinary Christian; but he did so while bearing the weight of a double calling to authority and sacrificial death. The king as an individual would have been a source of blessing in his compact sphere; but the calling to be ruler made him a shining solar sign all the more beautiful in its descent into the encircling gloom, promising a new rising to come.

All of these are part of the compelling Imago Dei that Charles presented and presents to the world. But there is the fourth. We began by affirming piety in the modern condition. Charles in his highly public but also personal way, showed how to practice this virtue of worshipful attention to each . In his devotion to God, family, and people during the tribulations of the early modern epoch, he showed the possibility of faith despite the forces of social and religious anarchy and breakdown. In him we see the possibility of a life in accordance with God despite all scoffing and persecution. And this experience allows one to encounter the contemporary not as a mere curse but as a condition for a heroic fidelity that not only remembers Jerusalem but rebuilds it, even out of the very stones of Babylon.

In the sign of the headless king, the restless heart with love is conquered anew.

THE QUEEN AND THE COMMONWEALTH

Frank Millard

We are broken as a country and as a nation. The glue, the fabric, the weft, and weave have been torn asunder. One person above all others united, not just the United Kingdom and the people she served around the world, but to a greater extent than we will ever comprehend, the world itself. She met and spoke with almost all of the global leaders since the Second World War and embodied the peace and aspiration that followed. We lived our little lives in the shadow of this giant, our second mother. Our poor country is bereft. We were nothing if not Elizabethans and honoured by being so.

As jubilee flags and bunting fluttered in the summer sunshine as they did in previous jubilees, we reflected on a life dedicated to our service. The period leading up to the jubilee had not been easy for our queen. Her husband died and she was forced to sit alone at his funeral on a day when government officials partied, Barbados rejected her as its queen, her grandson left the Firm and appeared with Oprah Winfrey in an infamous TV interview,

she caught COVID and two Royal visits to the Caribbean were marred by republican demonstrations and demands for apologies and reparations for slavery.

Meanwhile, for the enduring business of the Crown and Commonwealth, it was business as usual. On May 19, the Queen's Baton Relay reached St. Vincent and the Grenadines as the conclusion of its journey to all 72 Commonwealth nations and territories, bringing cultures and communities together in the lead up to the Birmingham 2022 Commonwealth Games, taking place from July 28 to August 8. It is that togetherness and common purpose which the Queen has represented and sought to promote since before her coronation.

Her Majesty made plain that the countries of the Caribbean held a special place in her heart—visiting personally in 1953, 1966, 1975, 1977, 1983, 1985, 1994, 2002, and 2009. She took her responsibilities as Queen of overseas realms, and as Head of the Commonwealth, very seriously.

The world is very different from 1952 and in spite of its advances, it is torn with division and injustice, the solving of which have been constant themes of Her Majesty's speeches from her Accession onwards. These expressions of her core beliefs, based on deep faith, include the unity of peoples expressed as family, peace, freedom, justice, common purpose, and an emphasis on youth and building for the future.

These days, however, duty has been replaced by accountability, an inculcation of honour with an assumption of amorality and a culture of modern blame confused with an assumed legacy of ancient guilt.

It is understandable, though unforgivable, that there are some people in Britain who regarded the Queen as theirs alone, plus some outside who also thought this was so. For the Queen, however, nowhere that, and no one who, had her as queen had any more of Her service or affection than any other. Similarly, the Commonwealth did not belong to the Queen, but the Queen most certainly belonged to the Commonwealth.

On her twenty-first birthday, she promised to dedicate her life to the service of her people of the Dominions and the Commonwealth her whole life

Royal Themes

On her twenty-first birthday, she promised to dedicate her life to the service of her people of the Dominions and the Commonwealth her whole life: "If we all go forward together with an unwavering faith, a high courage, and a quiet heart, we shall be able to make of this ancient commonwealth, which we all love so dearly, an even grander thing—more free, more prosperous,

more happy and a more powerful influence for good in the world—than it has been in the greatest days of our forefathers."

Following the death of George VI, Her Majesty spoke to Parliament of her determination to follow her father's example of devotion to the service of His peoples throughout the world: "I pray that with the blessing of Almighty God I may, ever justify your trust, and that, aided by your counsel and sustained by the strength of the affection of My peoples, I may uphold the ideals that My Father set before Me of peace, freedom and the happiness of the great family of which I am now the Head."

When she first became queen, she described the Commonwealth as an "entirely new conception" built on friendship, loyalty, and the desire for freedom and peace: "To that new conception of an equal partnership of nations and races, I shall give myself heart and soul every day of my life."

In 1952, she compared the Commonwealth to a family, which can be a great power for good: "A force which I believe can be of immeasurable benefit to all humanity" and described it as an "entirely new conception" built on friendship, loyalty, and the desire for freedom and peace. "To that new conception of an equal partnership of nations and races, I shall give myself heart and soul every day of my life," she pledged.

Later, at the time of her coronation, she spoke of the vast regions and varied peoples "to whom I owe my duty" and the living strength and majesty of the Commonwealth and Empire; of societies old and new, "Of lands and races different in history and origins but all, by God's Will, united in spirit and in aim."

She also spoke of living principles to be cherished and practiced, parliamentary institutions which she praised for their free speech and respect for the rights of minorities, and the inspiration of a broad tolerance in thought and expression. "All this we conceive to be a precious part of our way of life and outlook," she said.

She always referred to the past as the foundation and context of a living present and a future that we must all be active in building for the benefit of all people. She is the template for us all in her tireless devotion to duty already 36 years after retirement age.

She has not only worked hard, but put duty to her peoples and the Commonwealth above any personal consideration. In 1961, when after being cautioned not to visit to Ghana where there was civil unrest, she said: "How silly I should look if I was scared to visit Ghana and then [Soviet leader Nikita] Khrushchev went and had a good reception." Elizabeth also told her prime minister, "I am not a film star. I am the head of the Commonwealth—and I am paid to face any risks that may be involved. Nor do I say this lightly. Do not forget that I have three children."

Her Christmas speech of 1975 is particularly relevant today. She referred to great impersonal forces beyond our control, of brutal and senseless violence, and, above all, "the whole fabric of our lives" threatened by inflation, the "frightening sickness" of the world today as then.

For some, Her Majesty was a remote figure of wealth and privilege. For others a lady who would have loved to have just raised horses on a quiet farm a long way from celebrity and power. For others, she is the cornerstone of constitutions and defender of our democracy and freedom. She was, for certain, someone who gave her life for her people around the world and for those high principles to which the rest of us refer from a distance. She was the embodiment of the best of us and if we do not recognise that and cherish her service, maybe we never deserved it.

God Bless our late Queen and God Save the King.

KING CHARLES, 30 WATER BUFFALO, 3,000 HENS AND EGYPT

David Salter

On 6 May, Charles Philip Arthur George Mountbatten Windsor, His Majesty King Charles III, will be crowned in Westminster Abbey. Are we interested? I confess—as a Brit who once lived in the USA—that I am. But if you disagree, please don't stop reading. Charles is already King and Head of State of the United Kingdom and 14 other Realms—including such big ones as Canada, Australia, and New Zealand. He is also Head of the Commonwealth, with its 56 countries and 2.5 billion people. He inherited all this immediately upon the death of his much-loved and universally respected mother, Her Majesty Queen Elizabeth II, whose reign, at 70 years, was the longest in British history. Hers is surely an extremely hard act to follow—not that Her Majesty's faith and dedication to her duty was a mere act. I met her once and we had a lovely chat, making me late for another meeting. My best excuse ever for being late! Now,

I have every confidence in our new King. He's a really good chap. And I am only slightly biased because he bought me 15 water buffalo and 3,000 hens, helped me extend a school for tiny children in Egypt, and has been kind enough to exchange personal letters with me. Of course, none of us is perfect, and neither is our King. But I believe he has learned a great deal from his tough and rather lonely childhood, his failed relationships, and from being an amazingly far-sighted and tenacious prophet of environmentalism. He has had a long and detailed training to be an excellent King, and I believe he is already putting that into practice. Definitely someone we Brits (of a certain age) can call a Good Chap.

Going into history, we previously had King Charles I, who caused civil war and indeed bloody revolution in Britain long before France and the USA thought of such things. We cut his head off. Later his son, Charles II,

Artwork: *The Great Sphinx and Pyramids of Gizeh* by David Roberts, 1838 also known as the Merry Monarch, had himself a fine old time but did little good, in my opinion—other than in 1660 founding the Royal Society, the premier society for world-class scientists. These Kings were not great precedents, and many thought that when our current Charles came to the throne he would take the name George VII in honour of his serious-minded, diligent and shy grandfather, who saw us through World War II before tragically dying young from cancer. But Charles III it now is.

In view of the previous two, His Majesty is certain to add lustre to the brand. King Charles III is a serious-minded man with an amazing memory (like his mother, our beloved late Queen). Charles studied archaeology and anthropology at Cambridge and he remains interested in diverse cultures and the potential synergy between them. He has interests not just in his Christian heritage but in Islam (specially the Sufi tradition) and indeed also in much more esoteric areas, explored in his book *Harmony*. All this—and his late father, HRH The Duke of Edinburgh—has encouraged his active involvement in environmental conservation and indeed cultural conservation. I could write much about this. But others have already done so very extensively, and I suspect you want to hear about water buffalo, hens and schools for tiny tots. So let me take you to Egypt.

It was 10 years ago, 2013, and I have never seen such a thing before. A man is plodding along the seafront, blowing a warbling trumpet. He is carrying two big bunches of balloons, one at each end of a wooden pole across his shoulder. Is this man crazy, or just trying to sell balloons, or both? Selling balloons seems pretty odd, because it's already dark. And the streets are almost empty because a night-time curfew is beginning. Yet here he is, walking slowly. He's either crazy, or

extremely motivated. Menacingly, seven tanks rumble past to enforce the curfew, and the man speeds up a little. He blows his warbling trumpet again. Is he desperate? He's certainly brave. I am sure this brief glimpse will stay fixed in my memory—the determination and optimism of an honest man trying to feed his family. So this is Egypt, proud land of the Pharaohs, in October 2013. I return to fend off the biting spiders in my dimly-lit hotel room. And to risk drinking more of the tap water, because that's all there is. A lot lies ahead…

I have begged some time from my family and my (largely irrelevant) "day job" back in England to come to this land, whose history and culture I have loved since I was a boy. My maybe-mad idea is to offer friendship and some help, at a time of massive civil and religious instability, to the resilient and faithful Copts, those ancient Christians who are proud to be in the direct line of language and culture from the people ruled by the Pharaohs. Why am I here? Good question. I am British, not Egyptian. An ordinary Church of England layman, not Coptic Orthodox, and trained as a scientist, not a diplomat, priest, or journalist. I speak my native Devonshire version of English, and sometimes still passable German from my three years working in Hamburg, but only quite limited Arabic at this point. So why come to Egypt? Basically, because I couldn't get out of my head the idea of getting involved here. Nearly 40 years ago, having graduated in physics and mathematics, I was absolutely one-hundred-percent convinced that I should retrain in medical subjects. So I did, at London University's Medical College of the Royal Hospital of St. Bartholomew, founded in 1123—before the University of Oxford! I then went on to complete a research doctorate at Oxford, a master's in moral philosophy, and an international career in healthcare with a strong interest in anthropology and culture. Now, for the first time in decades, there is that same strength of conviction again. No fire-writing on the wall, or any mystical experience, much as I might have wished for it. Just a relentless motivation to *do* something, something that would begin a fair exchange, a genuinely two-way partnership, demonstrating and increasing respect on both sides. This would be really stretching across the international divides of language, culture, tradition, and a million possible misunderstandings. And I'm well aware that I'm not specifically trained. Just a man with some relevant experience and a very noisy bee in his bonnet.

When I had persuaded my family to join me on a holiday to Egypt late in 2008, I had absolutely walked on air through the famous Egyptian Museum in central Cairo. I was finally seeing some things—and even Pharaohs—who actually felt like old friends from my years spent reading their histories and peering at their pictures in Egyptology books. It was unexpectedly emotional. I probably wore a foolish grin throughout, as also when visiting Djoser's pioneering pyramid at Saqqara, reading hieroglyphs in Ptahhotep's beautifully-carved tomb nearby, stooping with hair-raised awe down, along and up the ancient corridor to reach the sarcophagus chamber of Khaefre's pyramid in Giza, and studying painted tombs in the Valley of the Kings. I had, after all, been the first translator of the hieroglyphs on a coffin in our local museum which had been there for 90 years. The owner, Iyhat, a *wab* or

> **The owner, Iyhat, a *wab* or purification priest, would I'm sure have been pleased to have his name and those of his parents recalled at last.**

purification priest, would I'm sure have been pleased to have his name and those of his parents recalled at last. But staying with my family in splendid hotels in Cairo and Luxor, though marvellous, can all too readily give the false impression to locals outside that foreigners are amongst the super-rich, which is not usually true in their home countries. And nice hotels shield the foreigners from what some call "the real Egypt." Not good—*mish kwais*! Personally, I wanted to see not the pre-interpreted tourist version, but the real Egypt, the more than 7,000 years of known culture beginning with prehistoric paintings in the lonely *wadis* of the Eastern Desert, and continuing in the faith practices and folk customs of today.

Earlier in 2013, I had watched TV reports of huge public demonstrations and civil unrest developing in Egypt. Mosque sit-ins were being forcibly ended by security forces, and literally hundreds of church buildings were being burned out by Islamic extremists, who either wrongly thought that it was Christians who had attacked the mosques, or believed—correctly but unjustly—that Christians were easier targets for revenge than was the Army. In nationwide chaos, both Muslims and Christians were killed, and a courageous Muslim saved Christian children from an orphanage set on fire by Islamist fanatics. Trying to describe all this, international media often focussed on burned-out church buildings because they outnumbered the damaged mosques. The burned-out churches of Egypt reminded me of the Minster Church of St. Andrew in my native city of Plymouth (the original one in England), built by Roman Catholics in the fourteenth century and for the past five hundred years housing a congregation of the Church of England, of which my family and I are now part. In the destruction of Plymouth's whole city centre by the Nazi's Luftwaffe in 1941, St. Andrew's was burnt to just a roofless shell. But having also lived in Hamburg in Germany, I was reminded of the massive destruction wrought there too by Allied bombing causing the terrible firestorms of 1943. I knew how, on both sides of that conflict, there had been irreparable loss of life, but places of worship had been lovingly rebuilt, and were once again buildings where prayers were prayed, songs were sung, and eternal life beyond the present world brought back to mind. That restoration had needed not just faith, but hard work and money for the reconstruction. So maybe we "rich foreigners" could help now in Egypt? After all, much of the Christian faith depends upon what happened in Egypt. There are many more examples besides, but just think of some from within the Bible. Consider the so-called sojourns, some bad, some good—indeed, some absolutely vital. Think of Joseph, who became number two to Pharaoh and saved his entire family from starvation, the family who soon became the tribes of Israel. Think of the "Flight into Egypt," when the Holy Family, taking refuge from their own country, were helped to save the infant Saviour. And there are the Desert Fathers of the early church, whose wise words and tough lives are still studied and cherished today.

Thus was born my "two-way partnerships" inspiration. Most Christians in England have more money than most Christians in Egypt. But most Christians in Egypt have, it seems to me, a more resilient and lively faith than most Christians in England, who tend to have "cooled off" somewhat due to....

what? (Insert your own ideas here!) So maybe a genuinely two-way, and thus *fair*, exchange could rebalance things and also produce significant synergy, a building up of the Body of Christ in which resources, spiritual and material, are identified and relocated to where they are needed most. I was reminded a bit of liver biochemistry and the physiology lectures in my student days at Bart's Hospital. Surely this idea was worth trying?

But it would not be comfortable in the way it had been while staying as a tourist in lovely hotels. On my Egyptair flight to Cairo, I was handed the several Egyptian newspapers I had asked for. Good to help learn the language, I thought. Yet I had not expected the front-page pictures of a sweet little 8-year-old Coptic girl, Mariam Ashraf Messia, cruelly and fatally gunned down just the day before by drive-by extremists. She was innocently waiting outside a church in a poor district of Cairo for the bride to arrive for her wedding. Mariam was just a little girl happily wearing her best clothes. She had asked her uncle to take a picture of her wearing them. And this child killing was deliberate. It was simply murder. Mariam was taken from her family and from life not by a stray shot, but by 13 bullets fired straight at her, "into the heart of Egypt," as the paper put it. I have three daughters myself, my youngest then being only twelve, and my memories of all of them came flooding back. I was so shocked by the unrestrained blind hate shown against this entirely innocent little girl that quite a few tears came to my eyes. They come back even now, many years later. And poor harmless little Mariam was not the only victim of that attack. Three others were killed immediately—a girl of just 12, like my own daughter, and two adults. Eighteen other Christians were wounded, including Mariam's mother, father and 3-year-old little brother. Also wounded were three Muslim guests, one of whom died of his wounds later. Did the hate-crazed terrorists know, or care, that these Christians were welcoming Muslim guests? And could those guests justify murder by others claiming to have Islamic faith? I doubt it.

Now all that was in the recent past. When daylight came after the balloon man and the tanks had gone home for a while, I found myself looking out at what the ancient Egyptians called the Great Green, *uadj-uer*, to me the rather beautifully blue sunlit Mediterranean sea. I was in Alexander's triumph and Cleopatra's capital, Alexandria, *Iskandria*, the greatest centre of learning in the world some two thousand years ago. Alexandria was the source of amazing new science. Here Euclid revolutionised theoretical geometry with the mathematical theorems in his *Elements*, whose lines, triangles and circles have been grappled with in schoolrooms ever since; Eratosthenes revolutionised practical geometry by measuring the radius of the globe (embarrassing flat Earth believers, but not eliminating them), and Aristarchus put our planet into its proper place orbiting the Sun, eighteen hundred years before Copernicus. Here, Herophilos was the first to conduct anatomical dissections in public and declare the brain to be the seat of intelligence. People used those very intelligences in Alexandria to make this extremely cosmopolitan city a melting pot for philosophical and theological debate between its Greek, Jewish and Egyptian residents. It became the home of, among others, the Church Fathers Clement and Origen, Plotinus and the neo-Pythagoreans, followed by gnostic "Hermetic" philosophers who laboured at what we now call alchemy, leading eventually to scientific chemistry. Seafarers were guided into safe harbour by Alexandria's innovative and massive stone lighthouse, the Pharos, one of the Seven Wonders of the Ancient World. Now, however, I had very respectfully tiptoed in as well, into this great city which had clearly seen better days. I was here, at the invitation of relatives of friends, to attend another Coptic wedding. But a very modern cloud had appeared on that blue horizon. The church booked for the wedding was mentioned in a terrorist hit-list, just discovered and discussed by local newspapers. Some priests were saying that weddings could, and maybe should, be postponed, thinking of the recent massacre at little Mariam's church. Indeed, in the bride's parents' flat I heard a very worried discussion as part of the pre-wedding family gathering. But Coptic faith and cultural resilience won through, and I attended the wedding, which proved to be joyfully noisy, as did chasing the bride and groom on a mad drive along Alexandria's seafront, the Corniche, in an open-topped sports car! Happily, the couple have flourished and grown into a healthy family with healthy children, and they are good Facebook friends of mine to this day.

In the following 10 years, a unique adventure has developed to personally involve, and be commended by, the Primates of two worldwide churches — the Most Reverend Archbishop of Canterbury, Justin Welby, and His Holiness Pope Tawadros II, 118th Patriarch of Alexandria — as well as HRH Prince Charles, Prince of Wales, now of course His Majesty King Charles III, plus UK Parliamentarians of both Houses at Westminster, civil servants at Whitehall, Universities, schools, church congregations and others. The ripples are still spreading outwards both in England and in Egypt, a significant sign of hope for the future in these very difficult times of pandemic, war crimes, climate change, population pressure and economic uncertainty.

Everything began in 2013 with that persistent idea about two-way partnerships. As I wondered exactly what to do, a Church of England curate and a Coptic Orthodox priest independently advised that I should, if at all possible, go to Egypt myself, to avoid unknown intermediaries and wasteful overheads here and abroad. They said I should find out directly where the need was greatest, and report back having gained authority for what I could report by being an eye-witness myself. So I spoke at St. Andrew's, we raised some donations for me to take, I took time off from my family and my day job, bought myself a ticket, and flew to Cairo. After finding a taxi and battling the famously hectic local traffic, I negotiated my way past two tanks and many soldiers at the steel-gated entrance to the walled compound of the worldwide head of millions in the Coptic Orthodox Church, His Holiness Pope Tawadros II. This compound was the Coptic equivalent of the Vatican. The Papal Residence in Cairo was inside this area, together with the great Cathedral of St. Mark and several smaller church buildings, although, sadly, all this impressive security did not stop the later suicide bomb attack and dozens of deaths in Boutrosiya church beside the Cathedral on Sunday, December 11, 2016. That attack of course was still in the future, as were many more besides.

Finding the Residence, I was allowed in to take a seat. After some six hours of waiting, Papal staff took pity on this entirely unexpected (and let's admit it, fairly clueless) foreigner hopefully holding a letter of introduction. They asked me who I was and why I was there. Then, unknown to me, they reported my presence directly to His Holiness himself, and he, most unusually and kindly, invited me to a lengthy private audience that very evening. The whole story merits fuller telling, and His Holiness surprised me by saying that we in Plymouth, in distant England, were the first to propose this idea of two-way partnerships, which he said showed "great love for the people of Egypt." This was very moving indeed in the circumstances, and I had to stiffen the sinews somewhat, despite being a buttoned-up Brit! His Holiness heartily commended this proposal and said that he would ask his Bishops to arrange for me to travel all over Egypt, even though diplomats and media folk were highly restricted, and all rail travel was stopped because of the significant risk of ambush and attack. In the most dangerous areas, banned even to the BBC, I was therefore provided with a personal escort convoy of seven police vehicles and 30 men with submachine guns,

... I was therefore provided with a personal escort convoy of seven police vehicles and 30 men with submachine guns, led by a Police General in person.

led by a Police General in person. Later, when I was back again in England, the BBC phoned me to ask whether I could ask the Pope for similar access for their media professionals—and I had to say that foreign laymen cannot just "phone the Pope"! But everywhere, whether guarded or not, I was able to talk and record interviews with the highest and the lowest, in major cities such as Cairo, Alexandria, El Minya, and Sohag, and in smaller places too. Many of these locations are generally unknown to foreign tourists and are not visited by the media either. They are simply too dangerous. In following months, I edited down the 60 GB of video and stills I had taken with my little HD camera, despite lacking assistance with sound or lighting. I organized the material, wrote and recorded a script, and got native-speaker help with properly translating my Arabic interviews with people into English subtitles. Interviewees included His Grace Bishop Bakhom of the Middle Egyptian city of Sohag, who gave a calm but hair-raising account of being attacked in his own Cathedral by terrorists using massive butane gas canisters as rams to break down the doors. They then set fire to the building, leaving the gas canisters to explode like steel-clad grenades. In due course I made a one-hour film of my tour of Egypt and gave away over 70 DVD copies of it, which I made at home. Because of its unique material, I was asked to show this at Westminster to UK Parliamentarians from both the House of Commons and the House of Lords, and was relieved when some Egyptian guests said they thought it was indeed an accurate portrayal, which they could not have outlined any better themselves. I also advised Prime Ministerial staff at 10 Downing Street and the Foreign & Commonwealth Office (later FCDO) as to what I had seen. Baroness Caroline Cox, the former nurse and now cross-bench Peer and Devon-raised intrepid pioneer of international partnerships, memorably invited me to a Devonshire cream tea at the House of Lords, and said she would "spread the word." The next year, I returned to Egypt and was again welcomed by His Holiness in private audience. I gave him multiple copies of my unique film on DVDs and USB memory sticks, and he gave me gifts in return, including a Papal medal of St. Mark. To my even greater surprise, he gave me a marzipan statue of Jesus, which he pulled from the top of an Easter cake he had been given earlier that day. ("Ah! Dr. David! Take

this for your children!" he kindly said when he first saw me again). I protected this statue inside two cut-down water bottles as I carried it around in the relentless heat of the Western Desert throughout the following week. In future years, I would meet this most kind Primate again on his first Papal visits to Luxor and to England. Meeting him has always been more than just theoretically a privilege. As a member of a Protestant church, I am not used to calling anyone "Your Holiness," but with Pope Tawadros it feels—and I mean *feels*—entirely appropriate. Initially trained as a pharmacist and a factory manager, it seems to me that His Holiness is a most wise, learned, practical and humble man with a good sense of humour. All these gifts, and more, now benefit the Coptic Orthodox Church worldwide.

Later there would be extraordinary visits to various monasteries, including visits to an especially isolated and vulnerable one in the Western Desert south of the Fayoum. The route was across a 20-kilometer dusty, unpaved desert track along which on more than one occasion other pilgrims—men, women and children—would be literally martyred in cold blood because, when challenged by Islamist bandits, they refused to renounce their faith in Christ. I have travelled this same dusty and unlit track, weaving between boulders, by night as well as by day, and can now recall it unsettlingly well. More than once I have been warmly welcomed to the monastery by the Abbot, His Grace Bishop Basilios. On my very first visit, conducted there by my Muslim driver Mohammed, Abbot Basilios followed the example of Jesus serving his disciples, and to my initial considerable embarrassment served me himself with some very tasty lentil soup and fresh, monastery-made, flattened *aesh masri* bread. Later, I raised with him the delicate question of what, if anything, contemplative monks can do to combat hateful violence—something which seemed initially to be an unlikely prospect. His very moving—and personally lived—answer became crystallized in the title of the film I later made and showed to Parliamentarians: "No Need to Hate." To visit this dangerously isolated monastery, and even to stay there, was memorable. On one such visit, I was invited to join in worship with the monks right through the night. All through the long hours the service went on and on, in Coptic of course, a mixture of *koine* ancient Greek and the last stages of Pharaonic ancient Egyptian. Well after dawn broke again everything drew to a close, and we could go to a simple breakfast. Later I was told that the service had in fact been shortened (to only about six hours) because "we are in the period of rejoicing after Easter." Very different. Immersive. Not the quick few songs and sermon we usually settle for in the Church of England! But it was such dedication to holy lives that produced the Desert Fathers of old, and the beginnings of Christian monasticism within these lonely open spaces of the desert.

In 2016, I began staying with a family in a small mud-brick village in Upper Egypt, and I have seen many changes there in the years since. Besides learning about everyday life, I have visited agricultural and educational projects to assist poor communities, and later reported to both His Royal Highness The Prince of Wales and His Holiness Pope Tawadros. This led to an invitation to Clarence House, HRH Prince Charles (as His Majesty then was) being known worldwide for his active interests in community and interfaith development. The Prince of Wales later gave generous donations to two of these projects, and he has very kindly stayed in touch since. By this means the monastery of St. Pachomius (Deir El Anba Bakhom), near Luxor, was able to expand their agricultural training work and improve local nutritional standards by buying 15 more water buffalo and building a better-designed compound for the herd. Buffalo milk is creamy, nutritious, and especially beneficial to the often very poor children in the locality. Anyone who has not yet tried half-and-half tea with buffalo milk will be pleasantly surprised if they do! Also, the monastery of the Saints (Deir El Gidiseen), near the small but ancient town of Tod, was helped with their little primary school for poor children aged 3 to 8 from the local desert areas, who otherwise would probably get little if any formal education. The much-appreciated school has been enabled to double its roll to 150 children, assisted by three local teachers and a team of volunteers, and to hire a third daily minibus to transport the children over often considerable distances from their sometimes very crumbly mud-brick homes, to which their parents have kindly welcomed me for tea. El Gidiseen's chicken farm has also been expanded from 2,000 to 5,000 hens, and four young graduates now have new jobs there. For all this and more, thank you, Your Majesty!

Early in 2018, I had the idea of setting up a genuinely two-way partnership between this little Coptic Orthodox primary school at El Gidiseen, and a Church of England primary school in Plymouth. With cooperation from teachers, I gave several illustrated talks to the Plymouth children about Egypt, and when they were enthused about making some new friends, I composed a table-top-sized (A0) bilingual "Welcome" poster for the school to send to Egypt, together with colourful A4 "mini-posters" which individual children made. Teachers held up the "Welcome" poster in the playground, surrounded by children, and I delivered to El Gidiseen a photo of this, plus the original A0 and A4 posters. Hakim, the school carpenter, made a special billboard to display the giant poster and another billboard for the mini-posters. Both boards were proudly fixed onto the school wall, and then we had a little opening ceremony with all the children present. Everybody was very happy indeed and all of us applauded everyone else! I also took to El Gidiseen some simple English books, as they had only one before, and brought a range of dictionaries for the teachers. In my five-day stay I gave some simple English lessons, limited by my sometimes laughable Arabic, including teaching to this Christian school a four-line round called "I Love Jesus", sung to the tune of "Frère Jacques." Their "combined performance" of this was later broadcast by BBC Radio. It was the first time the children had learned anything more than a few words in English, their third language after Arabic and Coptic, and as their average age was only about six, they really did very well. The Egyptian children then prepared a giant poster and mini-posters for the children in Plymouth, which are now on a display billboard, filmed by BBC television, thus completing the exchange. In 2020 I delivered picture postcards from the Plymouth children to the little school at Tod.The friendship continues, and I visited again in 2022. I believe that children in both places will remember their "exotic friends" overseas for many years to come. One day, they may even tell their own children.

Besides BBC TV filming this, the Archbishop of Canterbury's Reconciliation Team put up a big poster about it at Lambeth Palace, as it is apparently the very first international, interdenominational primary school partnership, spanning thousands of miles, different languages and extremely different circumstances for the children involved. The Most Reverend Justin Welby, Archbishop of Canterbury and Primate of the Anglican communion worldwide, took a personal interest, and I was invited to meet him at Lambeth. Just like the Primate of the Copts, I found the Primate of the Church of England to be welcoming and encouraging, and a photo of us both beaming broadly was duly taken to prove it. Even more positively, international ecumenical school partnerships like this are now being considered for replication elsewhere.

In 2018, I also stayed at the gigantic annual Festival of Saint George (*Mar Girgis*) in the high desert on the way to Kharga Oasis. Allegedly more than two million people come to the six-day Festival, including many Muslims (due to Saint George sometimes being identified with the mysterious Muslim figure of *Al Khidr*). People can meet friends from all over Egypt, and often those from overseas too. Happy Ethiopians and Sudanese sing and dance outside their tents, and Coptic services take place all day and all night. Strange white birds fly overhead and are hailed as a sign from Heaven. There are thousands of home-made tents to live in, and hundreds of tem-

> **In 2018, I also stayed at the gigantic annual Festival of Saint George (*Mar Girgis*) in the high desert on the way to Kharga Oasis. Allegedly more than two million people come to the six-day Festival ...**

porary shops selling food, clothes and toys. As the wind blows, the "streets" make huge clouds of dust laden with assorted bacteria and viruses, so most first-timers get ill with curious diseases, including me, despite my (years ago) surviving a postdoctoral research fellowship in the Oxford Pathology Department. Risk arises in part because there are many bullocks and rams at the festival. These are sacrificed and the meat is given to poor people. You can—and I did—step outside your tent at night and run into a great steaming bullock tied up nearby. I also turned a corner one evening to find a man carrying a complete bullock's head, unintentionally doing a convincing impression of the fabled Minotaur. Scary! Ritual sacrifice, reminding us of the Old Testament, and indeed of all the ancient Middle East, is just one example of many as to how time-honoured cultural tradition is still valued highly in Egypt today. Tradition links generations, providing strength and hope in the face of whatever difficulties young and old may face, which are often all too numerous. In the modern rush for the "new," I think it is very wise not to discard this solid and helpful underpinning. It is a tap root delving into deep time, stabilising and nourishing the present and—potentially—the future too.

Perhaps the happiest times so far came just before the worldwide coronavirus pandemic put most things on temporary hold. Because learning-disabled young people in Egypt tend to have to beg on the streets, if male, or be kept at home, if female, they often and understandably feel unsettled and undervalued. In Luxor, a city of over a million people, there is very little provision for them, and, perhaps surprisingly, friends in Cairo say they are not aware of any provision at all in that megacity of over 20 million people. There is provision, in fact, but it is not nearly enough. Because I know some of these learning-disabled young people and their often needy families, in 2019 a new thought occurred to me, which Egyptian friends enthusiastically called "*fikra helwa*," فكرة حلوة, "lovely idea," immediately I raised it. So we have put this into practice by starting little "workshops" for the learning-disabled to make small, easy things together. *People enjoy making these things and both they and their families are proud of what is made.* I knew from my own three daughters that girls like to make elasticated bead bracelets, for example. So I bought thousands of coloured beads, many metres of elastic thread and 500 small biodegradable plastic bags, then designed 700 specially-printed small bilingual sticky labels. His Grace Bishop Eusap, the Coptic Orthodox Bishop of Luxor, graciously met me, discussed the project and warmly endorsed it. Workshop groups now meet in church premises every Saturday evening, subject to COVID-19 precautions. There were, immediately, huge smiles all round at our first session, and not just at my crazy-foreigner demonstration of "how to do it." We have deaf, dumb, deaf-and-dumb, Down's, anencephalic and other disabilities represented. Most attendees are Christian, but there are some Muslims too. Everyone is always very,

> **There were, immediately, huge smiles all round at our first session, and not just at my crazy-foreigner demonstration of "how to do it."**

very happy to meet their friends and to do something productive. Smiles became even bigger when the Hilton Hotel at the world-famous Karnak Temple agreed to display the bracelets in a shop in their beautiful marble-paved lobby, for sale to tourists at low cost, with a percentage being returned to encourage the young people who make them. Bracelets are displayed complete in their biodegradable see-through bags with colourful bilingual فكرة حلوة / lovely idea labels. Amazingly, the Hilton is charging no commission at all for helping us. This generous initiative may well be a world first, and is certainly very welcome support for a cause which we believe will be a continuing beacon of hope in the even more difficult conditions of the post-coronavirus, post-Ukraine-invasion world. Word is spreading about this initiative too, to Cairo and elsewhere.

In late 2021, was delighted and honoured to be invited to work as a voluntary advisor to the Egyptian Ministry of Health's General Authority of Healthcare (GAH), and especially their Research Hub. The GAH is the health services public provider under the new Universal Health Insurance system (UHI). Established in 2018, GAH currently runs over 25 hospitals and 150 primary care units and centres in 3 governorates (Port Said, Ismailia, and Luxor); and it is expected to run all the public health facilities across Egypt by 2030, as the UHI expands to provide high-quality services to all Egyptians. I visited Luxor in December and January 2022 to see my many friends there, and also to visit some GAH facilities to make a beginning on this further collaboration, which is progressing slowly. There were also discussions about a much-needed substance-abuse rehabilitation centre covering all of Upper Egypt, and possible international University links, which will depend upon extremely hard-to-get permission from various Egyptian Ministries.

In my experiences over the past 10 years comparing life in England with that in Egypt, I have many times thought back to what Dave Tomlinson wrote in his provocative book *How to be a Bad Christian*: "Many rich and famous people leave this world friendless, miserable and frustrated, while others who possess very little depart in peace, surrounded by friends and loved ones, knowing that their lives have had significance."

I believe His Majesty King Charles III, thinker, philanthropist and internationalist, will not leave this world friendless, as someone having lived a life without significance. Quite the opposite. Even those little children in Egypt can tell you so. So I say with feeling, joining many millions across the whole world, *God Save The King*.

THE CORONATION

Justin Newland

"A joyous, colorful procession headed towards the entrance of the Abbey. At its head, members of the clergy wafted incense into the chill midday air. A cleric dressed in a bishopric hat and claret regalia led a young woman.

Proud she was and regal in her bearing. She had sequins sewn into her white dress and wore a fine coronet of jewels. The woman was Elizabeth, the daughter of Henry VIII and Anne Boleyn. She basked in the cold, high spiritual light of the Abbey. It was her coronation."

This is an extract from a novel I'm working on set in Elizabethan times. It's a great introduction to the coronation of King Charles III, due to take place at Westminster Abbey in London, England on Saturday, May 6, 2023.

The order of service of the coronation ceremony will be the same as it was in Elizabeth I's time. It's written and depicted in the medieval illuminated Latin manuscript, the Liber Regalis, and can be viewed in the Galleries at the Abbey.

Charles, like Elizabeth I before him, is again following the tradition of using Westminster Abbey as the site of the coronation. It was first used by King William (the Conqueror) on December 25, 1066.

A coronation is a powerful and evocative religious ceremony which culminates with the placing of a crown on the head of the sovereign. The root of the word coronation is corona.

A corona is defined as the rarefied gaseous envelope that surrounds the sun. It's an incredible sight, visible during a total solar eclipse. The imagery of a corona is suggestive of a halo, a bright circle of fire that both graces and illuminates. A halo is a ring or disc of light that often appears in religious art surrounding or above a person's head. It's a hugely significant mark of achievement in a savior or a monarch that indicates the person is capable of performing extraordinary acts of compassion, healing and leadership. What, one wonders, was the origin of the halo? Where did it come from? Did someone just decide one day to paint a halo around these people? Or did

Artwork: *Queen Elizabeth I* by unknown artist, ca. 1600-1610 someone actually see this ring of fire above a person's head?

For now, let's explore further the connection between a coronation and the sun. The sun's rays turn up here as a seven-fold influence—i.e. the spectrum of light from red to violet. So, it's not surprising to find that there are seven distinct parts to the Coronation Ceremony:

- The Recognition
- The Oath
- Presentation of the Holy Bible
- The Anointing
- The Investiture
- The Crowning and Homage
- The Recess

To begin with, it's interesting to note that the coronation takes place during the communion part of the mass. It suggests that the ceremony is a communion between the monarch and God and Godly powers.

During the first part of the ceremony—the Recognition—the sovereign stands behind the Coronation Chair and is presented to the people. He or she bows to all four sides of the Abbey – or the four directions.

The monarch then takes seven steps (seven again) up to the Coronation Chair which faces the high altar.

After the Oath and the Presentation of the Bible, the monarch is anointed with holy oil. This part of the ceremony is done in secret. A canopy is held over the sovereign because this, not the crowning, is the most sacred part of the service.

The Archbishop of Canterbury makes a cross with holy oil on the royal forehead, hands and breast. The tradition derives from the Old Testament where the anointing of Solomon by Zadok the Priest and Nathan the Prophet is described. It's no surprise to note that Handel's Zadok the Priest is sung during the anointing of the monarch.

The anointing is performed with olive and sesame oil with aromatic additions like jasmine and ambergris. The use of oil is fascinating in itself. Oil can be used to lubricate and insulate, but one wonders whether in this case it's used to symbolically seal a high spiritual power into the monarch.

The remaining parts of the ceremony—the Investiture and the Crowning and Homage— conclude the process. The Investiture of the monarch with the symbols of state is there to symbolize what's just happened, as is the Crowning. The Homage and the Recess are there to endorse and enhance. This uses the power of witness by those in attendance to strengthen what's gone before.

All in all, this is a magnificent ceremony, replete with hidden symbolic meaning, much of which is probably lost on us all today. We can still enjoy the sheer spectacle of the regalia, the ceremony, and the pageant, which has barely changed since the days of Elizabeth I.

Queen Elizabeth II on her Coronation Day
by Cecil Beaton, 1953

RICHARDVS X R ANGLIA II,

THE ENDLESS KNOT OF RICHARD II

Giovanni Costabile

"When Jesus therefore perceived that they would come and take him by force, to make him a king, he departed again into a mountain himself alone." (John 6:15 KJV)

In the year of Our Lord 1397, in the late night on January 5, King Richard II received three special guests in his secluded throne room, where he sat on the high throne in the only company of his Royal Guard and his close retinue, composed by his uncles the Dukes of Lancaster and York, his cousin the Duke of Aumerle, the Duke of Norfolk Thomas de Mowbray, and Richard's favorite, Sir Henry Green, Justice of the Peace. Richard's second wife, Queen Isabella of Valois, was only seven years old, so she had already gone to bed.

The first guest to pay his tribute to the King was a mysterious Jew called Rabbi Zohar. Not only were Jews banished from England for more than a century, but this special Jew was like a phantom whom everybody sought and none could find. Rumors had it that he was 500 years old, that he was the responsible for the Hundred Years War,

that he had caused the plague, and even that he had personally prevented the Crusades to achieve the final Christian dominion over Jerusalem. Any sensible Christian ruler would have felt compelled to execute the man without letting him utter one word, and instead Richard not only would spare his life, but he had personally requested an audience with the Rabbi. It was the Jew who was coming to Richard, but it was the King who needed the Rabbi.

"I have what you seek, Your Majesty," Zohar said, and he handed out a pouch from under his cloak. The Rabbi was old indeed, almost bald, with only a few strains of long white hair flowing down from his head like rivulets from Roman fountains. His eyes were blind, entirely white, and his skin was dry, smooth, only slightly wrinkled, as though some inner strength still preserved the bark of an old secular tree. The pouch was then brought before the King by two guards.

"Is it real, Rabbi?" the King asked, uncertain.

The Rabbi produced himself in a

Artwork: *King Richard II* by unknown artist, late 16th century disquieting smile. "As real as the Messiah, Your Highness."

Richard frowned. "We have different ideas about the Messiah, you and I, Rabbi."

Zohar smiled. "Indeed."

Richard raised a finger and the two guards unsheathed their blades.

The laughter of Rabbi Zohar filled the throne room, but, as the two Royal Knights advanced towards him, he excused himself. "Indeed we have different ideas about the Messiah, and yet we both are assured He is real."

Richard ordered the guards to halt. "Suppose I believe you, Rabbi. What is your price again?"

It was Zohar's time to shrug once more. "You do not have to pay me, Sovereign. You will have to pay God the Almighty."

"What does it mean?"

"You asked for the Wisdom of the Heart and you have it. Now prepare yourself to pay Solomon's price."

"Idolatry? Adultery? How dare you?"

The Rabbi laughed once more. "It is told that once upon a time Alexander the Great asked Diogenes the Cynic why did the latter live in a box, and do you know what was Diogenes's response?"

"What was it?"

"Move aside from there: you are covering the sun!"

Richard was wroth this time. "Seize that man!"

"Do, King, kill me. Indeed, I am dead already. And yet I live, because I know the secret you too shall now be a part of. Burn the precious alchemical library you inherited from your father

Edward, Richard, burn the *Almagestus* and the *Secretum Secretorum*! They avail of nothing, compared to my gift!"

The guards were uncertain whether to carry out the last order, and Richard told them to let Zohar go. "My best regards, Your Majesty," he said, bending his knee, before leaving.

John of Gaunt, the Duke of Lancaster, said, "Why are you letting him live, Richard?"

The King shrugged, then got up from his seat to personally collect the pouch the Jew had left. "You do not know what you say, Uncle. We should raise the Ban on Jews for what Rabbi Zohar just brought me."

Richard's cousin, Edward of Langley, inquired curiously, "What is it, cousin? What is it?"

Richard smiled. "This…" he started, but he was interrupted by the announcement of the second guest in that late night, a hooded man accompanied by none other than the Poet Geoffrey Chaucer.

The hooded man was silent, but Geoffrey announced him. "This, Your Highness, is the Poet from the West-Midlands I told you about. He composed three magnificent sermons in verse on the subjects of Purity, Patience, and Hope. He would rather keep his name and face unknown, though."

Richard was curious. "And why is that?"

The hooded man did not reply.

Geoffrey looked at John of Gaunt. "John," he said. "You can tell the King why."

Richard's uncle sighed, then he ex-

"What does it mean?"

•

"You asked for the Wisdom of the Heart and you have it. Now prepare yourself to pay Solomon's price."

plained. "Richard, this man was a priest, but he broke his vows and fathered a child with a woman he had fallen in love with. Then he lost his child, and made a vow never to show his face nor to speak to the living soul. He only communicates through his writing." Richard was impressed: "May I hear some?" Chaucer looked at the hooded man, who silently nodded. Then Geoffrey recited, in the original West-Midlands dialect of the unknown Poet:

Pearl of delight that a prince doth please
To grace in gold enclosed so clear,
I vow that from over orient seas
Never proved her I in price her peer.
So round, so radiant ranged by these,
So fine, so smooth did her sides appear
That ever in judging gems that please
Her only alone I deemed as dear.
Alas: I lost her in garden near:
Through grass to the ground from me it shot;
I pine now oppressed by love-wound drear
For that pearl, my own, without a spot

The King bade Chaucer to continue reciting, until he declaimed the whole poem. Richard was very pleased to hear how his initial impression that the pearl was the Poet's lost daughter was confirmed, and that the Poet had dreamed of her afterlife, thus being reassured in his own faith

The hooded man bowed to the King in sign of thanksgiving.

Then Richard said, "You are the right person to whom I can commission a poem. I want you to write a romance about Sir Gawain, based on the existing legends, that may work as a warning against adultery and a praise of marital fidelity. Geoffrey already wrote on this subject, and so did John Gower. Your own work would be highly appreciated, but make sure that Gawain's sign on his shield is Solomon's Pentangle instead of that stupid lion that some minstrels assign him."

The Poet nodded his assent, then

knelt before the King, followed by Chaucer. "By your leave, Your Highness."

Thomas de Mowbray said, "Your Majesty, I highly recommend not to admit the third guest in Your esteemed presence. The man is a rebel and a rascal, and such scum should not be allowed to dwell in Your proximity even for the best reason on this earth!"

Richard said, "The Kingsguard will protect me, I trust."

At these words, all the twelve knights surrounded the King's retinue. At that point, the third guest was introduced. He was none other than Henry Bolingbroke, the head of the Lords Appellant, the rebels who had tried to overthrow Richard's reign eight years earlier.

Henry made his defiant entrance without bowing to the King and even spat on the ground. "Surrounded by spears, Richard? Are you so afraid of a single man that you cannot hold your water?" Then he laughed, challenging the Court.

Richard said, "I could have you killed in the blink of an eye, Bolingbroke. But that is not the reason why I summoned you." "And what is that?"

"I want you to know that it is I who found it, as I was destined to be."

"That is not possible," said Henry, "for I am in possession of the original Ring of Solomon!"

And, by saying so, Bolingbroke put a ring on his finger, declaring, "I am already the King in the eyes of God."

Richard bit his lip, then he said, "I do not know what will happen to England after tonight, but I want you to know what will happen to me."

Bolingbroke laughed. "Are you going to finally let go of your bowels?"

Richard said, "Let us just say I have a little treasure too. Why do not we try and see which one is real? Are you not curious?"

The rebel considered the offer,

then declined. "It is surely a trick to steal my ring!"

Richard came forward, commanding the guards to step aside.

"Look, Bolingbroke," he said, extracting his own ring from the pouch where Rabbi Zohar had kept it. Richard put the ring over a brazier and let it fall into the fire. The flame turned blue, then green, then violet, then it went off.

Richard collected the talisman. "It is perfectly cold."

Bolingbroke frowned. "Well…" he started, then he put his own ring over another brazier, and let it fall there. The flame burned as usual, and when a guard collected Bolingbroke's ring from the brazier, what remained was only a melted piece of metal.

John of Gaunt, the father of the rebel, said, "Why do you not resign from your purpose to seize the crown, Henry? You are going to divide England in two factions!"

Bolingbroke was furious. "There have always been two Englands, father, at least since William the Conqueror set his foot on this ground! Or maybe it was Joseph of Arimathea who divided us when he told the Druids that we should worship a crucified man! But I will unify England, and there will be no rebels under my rule!"

Richard then spoke. "Bolingbroke, it is I who is going to resign. But you will have to win the Kingdom by force all the same."

Everybody was flabbergasted.

"What are you saying, Richard?" shouted Gaunt.

His son inquired, "Yes, what do you mean, Your Highness?"

He had spoken this last word as though it was an insult. Richard brought forth the Ring, so that everyone could see it, and he explained.

"The Ring of Solomon holds every power on this earth. There is nothing that a man cannot do by wearing it, since herein is inscribed the true Name of God, the Endless Knot that is Solomon's. And I have one use only I can think of for such a power."

"Why not to end the Hundred Years' War?" asked Edmund of Langley, the Duke of York, who had remained silent until then.

"Why not restore Jerusalem to Christianity for good?" asked Richard's cousin.

The King sighed, then said, "Because I am the King, and I am called to defeat. Such is my fate, whether I want it or not. Bolingbroke will be the next King. For within the hollow crown that rounds the mortal temples of a king, keeps Death his court. Or so will write a future Poet. But I am going to do something different, something that will ensure the survival of our Monarchy long after kings have become memories."

But I am going to do something different, something that will ensure the survival of our Monarchy long after kings have become memories.

"What is that?" all asked in unison.

Richard smiled. "I will walk into the Mists of Logres with my dead wife Anne of Bohemia, and watch over our Kingdom from the Once and Future Kingdom, where King Arthur lies in waiting. One day, I shall return with him and his predecessors, and those few among the Kings who came between us who partook of the same secret."

"Why?" asked Bolingbroke. "What is the secret?"

Richard said, "Only a few chosen

Kings become King of Logres. You will kill the changeling I will leave here behind me, but you cannot get into Logres. The way is closed for those like you!"

And, having said so, Richard was caught by a violent seizure. Even Bolingbroke was sorry for him, by seeing how the King was suffering. Eventually, though, the moment passed, and Richard opened his eyes once more, while the court physician inspected him.

"Green, my dear," Richard said, looking at his favorite. "What is Boling-broke doing here?"

What everybody thought to be appalling was that the fabled Ring was nowhere to be seen anymore.

Nobody ever heard again about Zohar the Jew, but the hooded Poet completed his commission and is today known as the Gawain-Poet after his most famous work, *Sir Gawain and the Green Knight*.

Bolingbroke did become the next King by the name of Henry IV, and the rest is history. Still, some say that even today, on the eve of the Epiphany, that is also the birthday of Richard, late in the night it happens to the current monarch to gather profound insight on some matter by listening to the wind blowing, and they call it "Richard's blessing from Logres," even when listeners do not understand what that means.

THE ROLE OF THE MONARCH

Alistair McConnachie

The job of the King is to reign, and in that work he performs two main functions:

Head of State

Unlike politicians, the King does not owe his position to a vote or vested interests. He is politically neutral and is untainted by everyday parliamentary turmoil and party politics. This means he can more easily represent all the people in a way that an elected President cannot.

If the Head of State is elected, people are less likely to look to him or his with affection. Half the country may oppose them! The president can become a divisive figure, and can end up being a scapegoat for the country's problems. This can breed cynicism, anti-politics attitudes, and even international opposition to the country itself.

As a politically neutral Head of State, the British monarch is able to provide a focused and tangible symbol of the people's sovereignty.

National Icon

The King is a distinct symbol of national identity. He represents the United Kingdom—the nation, its constituent parts, and the people—in a way that a transitory politician, who is here today and gone tomorrow, can never do.

When we look at the King, for example, we see more than Mr. Windsor. We see the embodiment of the national story of all parts of our Islands, stretching back through time, right back to Bruce and beyond.

The history of the four corners of the UK can be traced, dated, and discovered through the family history of the reigning monarch. He is a living link to our national story.

For some of us, the King and the Royals are also part of our own personal British identity; a way to identify with a larger community outside of ourselves.

Like a family, we grow old with these people in our lives. During the reign of the late Queen, she saw 15 different Prime Ministers. Most of us could only name a handful. The USA has had 14 Presidents. How many can we name? Yet in all that time, there was only one Queen. And we all know who she was!

So the monarchy is also about identity—national identity and personal identity—and the sense of place, the sense of self, the sense of belonging, which flow from these identities.

In this way, the monarchy conveys a sense of perpetual national continuity. When George VI passed away it was said: "The King dies but Britain lives on and a new Hand takes the Wheel of State." We said the same thing when Her Majesty passed away.

Through King Charles's children and grand-children, we see an assurance that this national story will continue into the future, and that the soul of the nation is immortal.

In an ever-changing nation and world, people are looking for symbols, icons of enduring identity and reassuring dignity. People are looking for constancy, for something which is faithful and remains, and is always here. In this way, the monarchy is a social unifier, and provides a social stability which a temporary politician cannot.

In an era of globalism, there is a tendency for countries to become the same. The monarchy emphasises what makes us different and interesting. It's a hugely significant cultural possession which makes Britain unique, colourful and distinct. To abolish the monarchy would be to abolish a vital part of our culture.

And for all its ups and down, it is also good that a family is situated at the centrality of British life. This esteems familyhood. And it's great value for money! The King and the Royals help us enjoy massive international goodwill. They generate economic activity wherever they go, and they are always helping to publicise good causes, and raise money for charity.

KING CHARLES III: THE ENTERPRISE OF THE CAROLEAN ERA

Charlie Keeble

The coronation of King Charles III will be an occasion of jubilation for the people of Great Britain and the Commonwealth. The last time we had a coronation was for Queen Elizabeth II in 1953, which happened in the middle of a very optimistic time. It was a brilliant year for Britain. We had just come off wartime rationing. Winston Churchill was prime minister yet again presiding over a changing nation. The DNA helix was recognised as the building blocks of living matter. Sir Edmund Hillary climbed Mount Everest for the first time in human history.

Our late Queen was anointed in the midst of optimism that launched a bold and brave new Britain, so can we expect a grand and glorious uplifting from our time of crisis and chaos with a new king? King Charles III has got a lot of potential to be a modern king and I am hoping that it will show through his patronage of classic designs and the natural environment. This I anticipate in reflection of his coronation em-

blem designed by Sir Jonathan "Jony" Ive, who famously designed Apple's unique computer products. It shows a crown made of the flowers of Britain's four nations.

When Charles became Prince of Wales in 1969, he declared in his investiture speech at Caernarfon Castle:

"The demands on a Prince of Wales have altered, but I am determined to serve and to try as best I can to live up to those demands, whatever they might be in the rather uncertain future. One thing I am clear about and it is that Wales needs to look forward without forsaking the traditions and essential aspects of her past. The past can be just as much a stimulus to the future as anything else."

Now let's paraphrase some of these words in the context of what he can be as king. Charles is determined to serve the people and live up to those demands. These demands are for the survival and hopeful aspirations that the British people need. I myself

Photo: *HM King Charles III* by Mark Tantrum for Governor-General of New Zealand, 2019 need a King that can be a voice of hope that can give me inspiration for prosperity in these dark times of uncertainty in the anglosphere.

There are moments of the past that Britain can be proud that King Charles can show us by example. Our former Queen showed resilience in the face of adversity and I followed that as a way of thinking about the strength I needed to endure a difficult time. What she went through during the war and the turbulent times of the monarchy tested her ability to deal with such matters. Charles intends to carry on the duty that his mother did and I hope that with his direction, we will be able to see through these difficult times as well.

King Charles has always been a staunch advocate of youth development and he has used his Prince's Trust to push for young people to make something of themselves. He has heaped praise on them for showing resilience and ambition in the face of adversity during the Covid pandemic. I can see that his support for empowering young people shows that we have a king that will make a shining light out of Britain onto the world's stage.

There is another aspect of Charles's interests that I find remarkable that suits British culture. He detests modernist architecture and is a keen supporter of environmental issues. I agree with him on these things. There are certain aspects of the past that are favourable to guiding us to the future. Looking after the environment and conserving the character of the British state in its architecture and natural wonders would be the way forward for the country.

In 1989, the Prince of Wales published a book called *A Vision for Britain*. In it, he criticised the way London was built without proper town planning and the way the postwar architects produced "ugly, concrete jungles that were completely without soul." This is exemplified by the appearance of the concrete skyscrapers that I grew up around in Central London. They look like monuments to Marxist unimaginative brutality. Buildings should have integrity just like people. Like people they should also blend in with their natural surroundings and stand out when they have extraordinary gifts.

King Charles demonstrated his ability to build a better town in Dorset with Poundbury, which is built in mind for minimal car usage and for people and businesses to be integrated into its design. King Charles, prefers in his words, "buildings that have grown out of our architectural tradition and that are in harmony with nature." The town's construction began in 1993, and it's scheduled for completion next year. What Poundbury has shown is that we must also grow our country economically alongside the environment and continue to support innovation and creativity.

I have been a long standing supporter of the monarchy and I love the Royal Family. They have provided a rock for the British people to hold onto their character and make Britannia a unique sceptred isle. I believe the monarchy makes me a merry member of an island nation that has produced so much in freedom of enterprise and invention. King Charles will be

King Charles, prefers in his words, "buildings that have grown out of our architectural tradition and that are in harmony with nature."

undertaking an enormous amount of responsibility and ambition to direct Britain into the future. He can count on me as a noble servant to do my duty for his kingdom, as I do through my advocacy work for the Commonwealth Games and for the UK Parliament.

When King Charles III is crowned this will be the first coronation of my lifetime. There will be celebrations in my town of Romford, and I will be enjoying the festivities with my friends. My MP Andrew Rosindell is a staunch royalist and likes to host Royal themed parties at his work office that is called Margaret Thatcher House. We will enjoy having celebratory parties for the coronation with plenty of drinks and food all around. We British do take pride in the pomp and circumstances of royalty. Rule Britannia and God Save the King.

THE FORGOTTEN CANONISATION CAUSE OF KING JAMES II

Charles A. Coulombe

My past remarks on the possibility of Charles I's sanctity awoke something of a hornet's nest. Not surprisingly, Ordinariate folk in particular were harshly divided, and a number of English-speaking cradle Catholics were simply outraged. It is interesting to note that Francophone Catholics (notably Bishop Bossuet, Louis XVI, and Fr. Jean Charles-Roux) often take a decidedly more positive view of the question—the latter named going so far as to serve as a patron of the Society of King Charles the Martyr and to write a pamphlet asserting the murdered king's sanctity in no uncertain times. Indeed, I remember a time not long ago when all but one of the SKCM's patrons were "Roman" Catholics.

Today, one of the highest-ranking Catholics in the Kingdom, Lord Nicholas Windsor, remains a patron of the Society. He has written, "In the King's personal piety, devotion and support of the Church, his ecumenical understanding (far advanced for his day), his patronage of the Arts in the service of God, his inspiration of the Christian classic, Eikon Basilike and of course his martyrdom, we have much to REMEMBER and be thankful for."

Now, other than objections that were actually addressed in the article, the two major ones that surfaced were a) that Charles never ceased to be head of the Church of England; and b) that he was crowned by the Archbishop of Canterbury and took the coronation oath. But a great deal of light may be shed upon these topics—and what Rome was willing to tolerate in those days, by looking at the career of his son, the indisputably Catholic James II.

The Servant of God, James II (so we must call him, since his cause was opened by the Archbishop of Paris in 1734; it may be dormant but has never been closed—and boasted at least 19 miracles at the time it was opened!) officially converted to Catholicism in 1670 with his wife, Anne Hyde, after

Artwork: *Portrait of King James II and VII in armour as Duke of York (1633-1701)* by John Michael Wright, 1660s

a fairly immoral life. Their daughters, Mary and Anne, later successively to usurp the throne, remained Protestant. James's wife died a year later, and he remarried in 1673 to the Italian Princess Mary of Modena. He assumed the throne on his brother's death in 1685, and the birth of a son precipitated the first successful invasion of England since 1066.

He went into a holy and prayer-filled exile in France, dying at St Germain-en-Laye in 1701. Almost immediately miracles began to occur at both his temporary resting place at St Germain, and his more permanent one in Paris at the English Benedictine St Edmund's Church (now the Schola Cantorum of Paris—the chapel survives, although the body was destroyed at the Revolution). The English Benedictines became custodians of his memory and offered prayers and so on for his canonization. The horrors of the French Revolution led to the Servant of God's cause going on the back burner; regardless of whether James is ever canonized, there can be no doubt of his Catholicity.

His coronation is the key point here, however. Although James II did not receive Communion during the Coronation Rite (having done so with his queen the previous evening at Mass at Whitehall), he did swear the same oath his father swore, with the Pope's permission: "Will you grant and keep, and by your Oath confirm to the People of England, the Laws and Customs to them granted, by the Kings of England, your lawful and Religious Predecessors, and namely, the Laws, Customs, and Franchises granted to the Clergy, by the glorious King St Edward, your Predecessor, according to the Laws of GOD, the true Profession of the Gospel established in this Kingdom, agreeable to the Prerogative for the Kings thereof, and the ancient Customs of the Realm…"

He responded, "With a willing and devout Heart, I promise and grant my Pardon, and that I will preserve and maintain to you, and the Churches committed to your Charge, all Canonical Privileges and due Law and Justice, and that I will be your Protector and Defender to my Power, by the Assistance of GOD, as every good King in his Kingdom, in right ought to protect and defend, the Bishops and Churches under their Government."

From that moment, with Papal approval, the Catholic King James was head of the Anglican Churches of England, Scotland (the latter would revert to Presbyterianism upon his overthrow), and Ireland. He was then anointed and crowned by the Anglican Archbishop. In exile, James acted as head of the English, Scots, and Irish Catholic institutions scattered around the Continent; but he and his son, James III, and grandson, Charles III, continued to be recognised as rightful sovereigns and heads of the Church by the so-called "Nonjurors"—Anglicans who refused to accept the new order of things. One of the few remnants of this headship of these Protestant churches by the Catholic Stuarts is the Protestant cemetery in Rome where Keats and Shelley are buried—and which was created by James III in 1716.

But this is not the last example of a Protestant Church being headed by a Catholic. The Protestant churches of Bavaria, Saxony, and Austria were all headed by their respective Sovereigns. In the last case, for two years it was Bl. Emperor Charles of Austria. As noted in the last article, he resembles the British Charles in his role as family man; here is another point of resemblance! At any rate, as shown by his son James II, Charles I's coronation by and headship of the Church of England need not be an impediment to his eventual canonization—if, of course, he is indeed in Heaven. 🍂

King David playing the harp
by Gerard van Honthorst, 1622

Fellowship & Fairydust

COUNTRIES, NATIONS AND PEOPLES — THE ENGLISH MONARCHY: A REVOLUTION

Stephen Fry

Forgive me, I am English! I was born in the County of Middlesex (which no longer exists). I live in Surrey, England, which apparently is part of a State known both as the United Kingdom and as Great Britain. I am not Scottish. I am not Irish (part of the British Isles but only the northern counties are part of the United Kingdom)—stay with me—and I do not feel British; because I do not understand what that means. For the purposes of my attempt at recognising what my nationality is, the Principality of Wales is not a country. I am of the people. I hold the franchise afforded to me by the freedoms of democracy. I am naturally a radical, a conservative a libertarian; perhaps.

All the above came whistling into my mind as the uncoded British Constitution was rolled out for all to see as the days similarly rolled out following the death of our late Sovereign Lady, Elizabeth. Presented on television as a spectacle, an odd group of happenings where people used interesting language, wore even odder clothes, blew trumpets, marched in grand military liturgy. That was happening? The British Constitution is not written down, as I mentioned above, the Union exists as a tension of relationships: The Palace of Westminster, Parliament; the Law Courts, the Judiciary; the Palace of Lambeth, the English Church; the Military—all operating in a substantive balance or tension of checks. All held together by the Monarchy, the person of the Sovereign. As an aside, for a moment, government ceased to exist with the death of Elizabeth. Power was transferred to the Privy Council to note the accession of the new king; after which the machinery of government had to make a fresh declaration in recognising a new Sovereign and thereby being allowed by this tension to continue its work in government. All very odd in a democracy—the people choose—but nonetheless even the franchise is checked with balances of

Photo: *King George 1923* by Bassano Ltd, 1923

the establishment. Imagine the surprise for those who listened to the acclamations, the declaration of the new king by the Heralds, to discover that London is not part of the United Kingdom! Seriously? Ask why the Monarch must yield to the Lord Mayor of London as they enter the City. All of this is the wonderful mystery of the English Monarchy that binds a people, a state, a system with only one aim, to protect and defend the Monarch and the Peoples of the realm.

Step back in time with me. George V; George Frederick Ernest Albert of Saxe-Coburg and Gotha; June 3, 1865-January 20, 1936. He led the paradox of the Royal Revolution in 1917. It is this action that saved and gave us the monarchy we have in 2023. He was profoundly conservative, devoted to regular routines. A great diarist. A hater of pressed, creased, trousers and turnups, no modernity; yet a revolutionary. Upon his accession to the throne in 1910, his view was maintained, ceremony and splendour, tradition and ceremony. The Coronation of George was, outrageous in its splendour—liturgically, musically solemnity—disciplined, organised, and rehearsed. Why? For the first time there was an understanding that the Monarchy was now watched by a new audience—the Peoples of the Realm. The Populus wanted to see, wanted to be involved, they wanted a good show, they wanted a performance. George gave them that; he was not a natural to this public display of kingship, but he was a conservative. George knew that the ceremony of State, acted by a king, by him was in fact his duty. This idea of duty became the touchstone and power base of monarchy, continued by George VI following the abandonment by Edward VII, and passed on to the psyche of Elizabeth II.

George was a democrat, as monarch, he presided over the divisions between the House of Commons and the House of Lords. He signed the Parliament Act of 1911 which destroyed the independence of the House of Lords. This meant that the Monarchy could survive as the aristocracy became replaced, drop by drop, of his new audience, the people. He celebrated the people by completely restructuring the great, enormous public space for people, in front of Buckingham Palace, who could greet their king and his people—Admiralty Arch, the Mall, the Victoria Memorial—a public piazza, a theatre for ceremony, for the engagement between people and king. All of this is George's interpretation of the continuum, originating from his father Edward VII, but emphasising his own understanding of people, power, authority, and constitutional tension. Edward VII had a great pride in friendship. His love of France (a new relationship) was similarly adopted by George and led a nation away from the revolutions of Europe—the falls of Russian, Germany, Austria, etc.—and into a war victory on the battlefields of Ypres. People and Sovereign, united by victory, united by the mobilisation of men and women in a just cause—attacked by demands for a republican society by H.G. Wells and other Fabian Socialists, and supported by the unmentioned stirrings of rebellion and mutiny with a huge rise in the casualty rates of a poorly orchestrated war. There was even a suggestion that George was......foreign—a man presiding over a dull alien Court! George becomes frightened, his rush to engage with his audience, the people, all seem to be failing. His sense of duty may not be enough. The first king to speak only English. His nerve was shaking, the Royal House was German. The marriage rules of the German Royal House required only marriages back in Germany! Every generation would re-Germanise the Royal Household, the Royal family, the next generation of Sovereign. George realises the problem. He sees a war with Germany, his own people. He realises that something must be done. He cannot end the war without a victory, he will not get a victory unless he ceases to be seen as a German. The Royal House must change its name and its Royal Customs. What should he be called? What would the people accept as an English name for an English king? Windsor is born. The Town is the seat of the Garter, it is home to legend, pageantry. The name is declared in Council. The whole Royal family are rebranded—Battenburgs are Mountbatten, Saxe-Coburg and Gotha is now Windsor. At the same meeting of the Council George declares that the marriage customs have changed, and the Royals will now marry English people. The summer of 1917 saw the end of a German dynasty and returned the Monarchy to a national possession, a family of the people. The way in which the relationship between the subjects, the people, the citizens are now integrated.

George has democratised the Palace of Westminster, Commons over the Lords. Government for the people, for the many not for the few. With this he created a new structure, an order; a reward open for the people. The new Orders of Royal validation, the first investitures, the OBEs the MBEs, the CBEs the Knights of the Grand Cross, all changed. All new, a new engagement and reward for the people. Populism was sentimental and public. The very first of a new Order, the innovation, was presented to the people in public. Not a Palace, not in Westminster, not in London; but in a sports stadium, Ibrox park, in Glasgow Scotland. The revolution, the Royal Revolution was complete.

Come back to 2023, now we have a new king, a new Prince of Wales, a slimmed down Royal family. All very English-looking now. All very populist, all very egalitarian, all very effective. Effective because of Queen Elizabeth promising at the beginning of her reign to follow in the footsteps of her grandfather, George V. The revolutionary king who was a conservative, ahead of the curve, discerning, informed, and well advised. The man who saved the monarchy and made it what it is today. His inheritor, King Charles III, a similar man, a man who listens, who acts, who speaks out for the people, a people's king; a man who understands the relationship between Sovereign and his Peoples.

THE ULTRA-ROYALIST

Jojo de Lenborough

During the recent mourning period of our most beloved Queen, I was asked by acquaintances if I am a royalist, to which my answer was always that I am a self-proclaimed "ultra royalist." This comment was often met with glee and comfort as people felt that they had found someone to confide in during those moments of sorrow. Brits are renowned to be reserved creatures who dislike bothering others with emotions. However, there are rare times where the procrastination of the potential embarrassment that can arise from displaying such feelings are foregone. This was one of them.

Of course, my friends and family needn't ask my stance on the matter, as my blatant royalism is something that I have always worn on my sleeve. In fact, I only found out about the dreadfully sad news when my phone rang as I was in the bath and a close school friend asked how I was coping. I had been worried all day about the inevitable having followed the news earlier.

My mother called next, checking how I was feeling, followed closely by contact from my brother, who was uncharacteristically shaken by the news and admitted to being quite distraught. He had emigrated to Canada some years ago and the connection of The Queen reigning the two realms he calls home had always offered him comfort and familiarity. He, too, like the vast majority of us, had felt that he'd lost a family member. Well, The Queen had really become the grandmother of the nation and her people.

The image of the many people crowding the roads to pay respect to Her Majesty all the way from Buckingham Palace to Windsor Castle will always be in my memory as one of the proudest moments I have ever had of my fellow Britons.

Indeed, I was taken by surprise to the point that I was greatly moved for days by how many of Her Late Majesty's subjects really did love her. Genuinely. I say this because, unlike anyone else I know, I not only displayed The Queen's portraits in my home and in my office, but I also always wore portraits of Her Majesty as lapel pins and as a necklace whenever I could. This, I believed, has earned me the privilege of being able to proudly label myself as an "ultra-royalist."

However, how I came to be so was somewhat lost on me until very re-

Photo: *Her Majesty Queen Elizabeth II, Queen of New Zealand* by Julian Calder for Governor-General of New Zealand, 2011

cently when I went back to Thailand for the first time since the coronavirus pandemic swept the world.

Thailand is a country that I have traditionally spent a month in every year since I was 13 years old and has greatly—often subconsciously—influenced my outlook in life. One aspect is definitely my love of monarchy.

I believe that standing along with everybody else for the Royal Anthem in the cinema before the film started was my monarchist awakening. Something about the absolutely beautiful Thai Royal Anthem accompanied with the imagery of the King reaching out to his subjects on a rainy day moved me so much that I remember that I started to cry. Never before in my 13

years had I been moved to tears in such a manner. I strongly recommend listening to the Thai Royal Anthem whenever you have the chance to see if you also feel the magic that entered into my very soul that day.

Alas, I cannot remember the film that followed, but I do remember being sat throughout forming within the dark and freezing cold air-conditioned cinema a love of monarchy in my mind. How wonderful it is to have a living and breathing symbol of nation and Her continuous history for all of the citizens, regardless of politics, race, or creed, to be united in support and love for!

After leaving the cinema I went on to really notice for the first time all of the portraits of His Late Majesty King Rama IX everywhere around the city with new and enlightened eyes: from large pictures on skyscrapers to small ones in the entrance of every shop and home. I also noticed many wearing images of their Great Beloved King Rama V as necklaces, who reigned during the Victorian period, renowned for the prosperity and advancement of Siam during his reign. Inspired by this, I, too, made an image of Queen Victoria and wear that as a silver necklace quite often. In fact, my love of these images has caused me to fall quite deeply in love with the British Royal Family Orders and I am quite excited to see what His Majesty the King chooses as his colour of ribbon.

Upon my return to Britain and with each trip back to Thailand, I have become more and more monarchist and have brought back with me more and more inspiration on how to promote royalism, monarchy, and love of our Sovereign. Because, it is through that very love, en masse, we can be a united nation and family of nations across the world. A global family under one Crown upon which the sun never sets causing eternal peace between us.

It is because of my belief in this that I have a pipe-dream that the Commonwealth Realms should become a single confederated nation. We are all one family loyal to our one true king. To be British should not be dependent on where you were born or what race you are, it's a state of mind: do you pledge loyalty and love for our Sovereign? If yes, you are British. It is the essence of what makes us as a people. The only defining characteristic or trait that binds us no matter where we are on Earth. You are one of us just as the Torah binds the Children of Israel across the planet.

The preservation of our Crown—a symbol of stability and strong defence from invaders—is something that has passed down from generation to generation of our people for over a thousand years and, like a link in a long British-forged chain, I feel it is my duty to preserve and defend the glory of our ancient monarchy for the next thousand years of Britons to enjoy, appreciate and feel proud of.

Now is time for the New Carolean Era and for me to love and treasure the images of Her Late Majesty but also replace them with our new king and queen. I already have had the opportunity to proudly sport my new lapel pin that I commissioned recently of His Majesty and it has been met with many compliments and even a doffing of hats.

I am ever so thankful to my fellow Brits for the outpouring of support and appreciation for our king as he begins the hard work and sacrifices that will burden him for the rest of his life for the good of our nations and peoples.

The privilege of being able to witness a coronation will be treasured by all who watch it for the rest of their lives and is set to be the most watched event ever in the history of television. Her Late Majesty's funeral is the current holder of that position. A record no presidential inauguration will ever hold.

Even though I will be watching on television, I shall stand along with those at Westminster Abbey and shout "God Save The King" three times as St. Edward's Crown is placed upon our rightful Sovereign's head and, I do hope that in a moment of global Commonwealth Realm unity—from Canada to Tuvalu—all of my fellow brothers and sisters across the world under The Crown do likewise, for unity and fellowship is exactly why we have our king.

MARY THERY (MARČA TERČA)

Martina Juričková

Slovak

There was a king, once upon a time,
Charles IV was his royal name.
He had three daughters and but one son
who died in childhood, so there was none
male heir left, just three princesses.
Such ordeal real unfortunate is.

The oldest daughter was Maria,
her second name was Theresia.
But some nobles who yearned for the throne
didn't want her to receive the crown.
Therefore, her father took an action
and issued the Pragmatic Sanction.

The greedy aristocrats were tricked
since according to this new edict
after Charles's death would Mary
become the queen of all Hungary
and other Habsburg dominions
and the nobles'd be her minions.

But some years before she came to reign
she fell in love with Francis Lorraine.
When they married, Mary was nineteen.
Later she bore him children sixteen.
Eleven girls and five princely boys
brought the parents many fears and joys.

Kde bolo, tam bolo,
tam bol raz jeden kráľ,
čo sa volal Karol
a štyri deti mal.

Keď mu jediný syn umrel,
s kráľovnou ho oplakali,
lebo stratil následníka,
len princezné mu zostali.

Najstaršia bola Mária,
Terézia ju volali,
avšak kráľovskú korunu
jej šľachtici dať nechceli.

Tak jej kráľovský otecko
vymyslel hneď taký zákon,
by Mária po ňom v Uhorsku
mohla raz zasadnúť na trón.

Tento zákon sa menoval
že Pragmatická sankcia.
Podľa nej celé kráľovstvo
tak zdedila Terézia.

Vo veku devätnásť rokov
sa za Františka vydala
a z veľkej lásky mu potom
šestnásť detí porodila.

Artwork: *Portrait of empress Maria-Theresia*
by Matthias de Visch, 1749

Two of them grew up to become kings.
Half of the others suffered bad things
which caused Mary many days gruesome.
But all that was only yet to come
when, twenty-three, she was crowned a queen
the kingdom had never before seen.

The striking coronation took place
in the town of Pressburg, that's today's
Bratislava in Slovakia.
At that time freshly queened Maria
couldn't have known what life had in store.
The first test of her rule was a war

with Frederick of Prussia over
Silesia, who wished to make her
give the land up. She was unwilling,
opting for seven years of battling.
Sadly, she lost it. But still she won
her subjects' allegiance from thence on.

She fostered enlightenment by all means.
Codex Theresianus, the queen's
set of laws revised land ownership
and unified court rules and judgeship.
She reformed health care and army, too.
In agriculture she proposed to

plant new crops like corn and potatoes.
She was the first to use money notes
in Europe to pay for goods in trade
and little children she by law bade
to attend school, get educated.
She made it a right of every kid

that they could learn some instead of, say,
working hard in the fields the whole day.
Mary outlived six of her children
and husband, too. That's why till the end
of her own life she wore mourning black.
She missed terribly her beloved Franck.

Probably a smallpox aftermath
led to Mary's eventual death
at the age of sixty-three, ending
thus her forty-year rule as a queen.
She was succeeded by her son Joe,
Joseph II who became known

Jedenásť diev, päť princiatok,
bolo potomkov kráľovských.
Vladármi sa neskôr stali,
na radosť matky, dvaja z nich.

Dvadsaťtriročnú ju v Blave
slávnostne korunovali.
Vtedy ešte netušila,
aké veci ju čakali.

S Fridrichom z Pruska o Sliezsko
mnoho vojen bojovala,
čím si u svojich poddaných
veľkú dôveru získala.

Terézia osvietenectvo
všemožne podporovala.
Armádu a zdravotníctvo
aj súdy zreformovala.

Práva a tiež povinnosti
zemepánov upravila
Tereziánskym urbárom.
Školský zákon stanovila:

Vraj každé dieťa v kráľovstve
má právo chodiť do školy,
namiesto aby celé dni
len pracovalo na poli.

Ako prvá v Európe
zaviedla v platbe bankovky
a ľudu kázala sadiť
kukuricu a zemiaky.

Že jej láska bola silná,
po náhlej smrti manžela
po zvyšok svojho života
len čierny odev nosila.

Za štyridsať rokov vlády
šesť svojich detí prežila.
Napokon na rozdutie pľúc
v šesťdesiatich troch zomrela.

Známy koncom nevoľníctva
a tolerančným patentom,
najstarší syn Jožko sa stal
mamičkiným nástupníkom.

for the Patent of Tolerance and
celebrated as the peasants' friend
for the abolition of serfdom
in the whole Hungarian kingdom.
Be sure this is no fairy-story,
there once really lived this queen Mary!

Kde bolo, tam bolo,
nie je to rozprávka!
Kedysi fakt žila
tá slávna Marika.

THE KING
AND HIS FAITH

Elliott Malik

An investigation into how the King's faith will affect his interactions with religion, including a preliminary overview of the history of monarch-state church relations and his constitutional role.

The King, the Constitutional Settlement, and the New Era

"The role and the duty of monarchy also remain, as does the Sovereign's relationship and responsibility towards the Church of England. The church in which my own faith is so deeply rooted." — from the first speech of HM the King as monarch

From Wessex to the United Kingdom, a golden thread has united our past, our present and our future. The monarchy has remained a focal point for all of us. Yet, during this time, the monarchy has transformed—from absolute to constitutional, Saxon to British, Catholic to Anglican. Throughout our history, the religious nature of the monarchy has been undoubted. From King Alfred the Great to King Charles III, our monarchy has always rested upon the sacred bedrock of the Church.

This settlement seemed sound, but it has been rocked by the recent move away from faith. The previous role of the monarch as the stalwart defender of the state church—and nothing else—seems to be in doubt. Indeed, the clamour for a separation of church and state ignores the serious constitutional ramifications for the monarchy.

Our king has his own beliefs, with a broader acceptance of other viewpoints being central to this. But he must work out how he will navigate this new era. Before an analysis of the King's own beliefs, and how he may navigate through the religious tumult of his reign, can be made one must examine the history of monarch-church relations.

From the Saxons to Modernity

Reaching back to the origins of England, King Alfred the Great identified his role with the sacred. He was not simply a king and warrior. He greatly supported the Church, believing it to be a bulwark against the "divine retribution" of the Norse invasions. He wished to act upon his belief that it was his duty to look after the spiritual wellbeing of his people. This continued throughout the Anglo-Saxon era, with the Church providing a foundation around which Wessex, then England, could coalesce. The number of Anglo-Saxon royals who joined the clergy—many of whom would be canonised—attests to the deeply religious nature of monarchy at this time. Equally, the toleration and acceptance of the Benedictine revival indicated that the monarchs were interested in new theological arguments, as well as wishing to ensure that the Church operated in the best manner possible.

The medieval period saw the Church's power being fully utilised by the monarchy. In this period, perhaps due to better documentation, the tensions between church and state grew dramatically. Initially, tensions were low, with King William the Conqueror acceding to many church demands—mainly due to the Papacy providing legitimacy for his conquest. However, the Church accepted the king as the ultimate authority over the Church, thus foreshadowing the conflicts of the future. Indeed, during the reign of King William II, cracks truly began to emerge. William II battled with Anselm, Archbishop of Canterbury, and this only settled due to the intervention of Pope Urban II. Through the reigns of Kings Henry I, Stephen, and Henry II, the balance between church and monarchy gradually deteriorated. The final act in this melodrama came with the martyrdom of Thomas Becket, Archbishop of Canterbury, in 1170. However, as all who have studied medieval history know, at this point the monarchy did not have the power to threaten the Church and its supreme authority. Rather, Henry II was

scourged by monks and prayed for a day and night in front of relics, before agreeing to restore all Church lands and privileges which he had removed.

The later mediaeval period saw a marked improvement in the relationship between the monarchy and the church. Beginning with King Richard I's crusades (and ignoring King John's unfortunate lack of piety), the institutions of church and monarchy were closely bound. This can be seen in the piety of Kings Henry III and Henry VI—Kings who even had miracles ascribed to them. Henry VI provides the image of a "Most Christian King." His impact upon mediaeval church art and architecture cannot be overstated.

Alas, all good things must come to an end. With the end of the mediaeval period came the end of the old order. The early Tudor era saw many similarities with the previous era, with Henry VIII being granted the title "Defender of the Faith" by Pope Leo X. However, his marital strife led to the greatest social, cultural, and theological cataclysm in this Kingdom's history: the Reformation. The relationship between church and monarchy collapsed, with the dissolution of the monasteries under King Henry VIII, and the Reformation reaching its Protestant peak under Edward VI. Whilst Queen Mary attempted to return England to the Catholic fold, this collapsed after her death. Only the reign of Queen Elizabeth I restored some calm, with a middle path being developed between Catholicism and Protestantism.

However, the Tudor period highlights an important aspect of the relationship between church and monarchy. The monarch did not need to obey the papacy to continue the merging of church and state. Rather, the English monarchy remained Christian and remained devoted to protecting the church—albeit this now being the Church of England, rather than the Catholic Church in England. The monarch would forever be the Defender of the Faith, with the Church being headed by—and defended by—the monarch.

After the tumult of the Tudor era, the Stewarts provided no respite. The era began promisingly, with King James I maintaining a steady ship. Puritanism was curtailed, an attempt was made to move the Scottish church closer to the CofE, and, most importantly, the greatest translation of the Bible in the English language was created. King Charles I continued his father's work, but with a horrific conclusion. The unity of the church and the monarchy did not lead to a resolution of religious tension. Rather, it ended with a Puritan military dictatorship ruling over the Three Kingdoms, and the martyrdom of the King. Following the restoration of King Charles II, the troubles continued. King James II—a Catholic—was exiled, and a Dutch Protestant (William III) was imported to rule.

During the Stewart era, several new threads were woven into the relationship between monarch and state. Parliament's role grew tremendously—with the Act of Succession ensuring that all Catholic claimants to the British throne would be excluded. Equally, the reign of King Charles the Martyr demonstrated the limits to the monarch's power to protect and enhance the church directly.

The Georgian era cemented Anglicanism as the state church. Never again would Britain be at "risk" of returning to the Catholic faith. But this did not involve the monarchy being particularly active, theologically. Rather, this was facilitated by the crushing of the Jacobite uprisings and the Whig supremacy. During this time, perhaps due to there being no theological weight, an explosion of new Christian sects emerged. This was the first chink in the monopoly the Church of England had over its people.

The House of Saxe-Coburg Gotha (latterly Windsor) has seen a continuation of this trend. The power of monarchy to influence the Church of England has waned, with no monarch publicly interfering in church affairs. This era has seen two important changes: the acceptance of different faiths and the explosive growth of atheism. Both have radically changed how the monarch deals with theology—even if through simple speeches. Whilst the Victorian era saw the last attempt by the establishment to stamp out religious dissent (the reaction to the Oxford Movement), the second Elizabethan era saw complete acceptance. Indeed, whilst Her late Majesty has become known as "Elizabeth the Great," her greatness came through the constant highlighting of the importance of her faith. Even as the British population has moved from being almost universally Anglican to an Anglican minority state, members of the royal family have continued to discuss the important role that faith— Christian faith—holds.

What does this mean for our King? Certainly, we can assume that the King will not be a warrior king like Richard I. Nor will he attempt to crush any non-establishment (i.e., not the Church of England) faiths, as Henry VIII and Charles I attempted to do. The King may decide to follow the examples of Alfred the Great, Henry VI and James I: reinvigorating faith by providing a new intellectual stimulus. However, this would have to be done privately. His kingdom will not tolerate "interference." In truth, it is likely that the King will continue as his mother did: discussing his faith, maintaining Anglican traditions, and demonstrating a keen interest in church matters. However, there will be one key difference. The King is profoundly ecumenical, and he will defend all faiths, even if his primary concern is the Church of England.

The King's Constitutional Role

The King is the Supreme Governor of the Church of England. As such, he appoints Bishops and Archbishops. Regarding the Scottish Church, the King must swear an oath to protect it and has the power to appoint the Lord High Commissioner of its Church Assembly.

However, these signs of power are, in reality, much reduced. The King appoints Bishops and Archbishops to the CofE on the advice of the Prime Minister. As mentioned, the King's powers are now titular. Indeed, the Scottish Church demonstrates this with acuteness. The Lord High Commissioner is purely ceremonial, not even having historical powers to influence the church.

The King will not seek to amend any of this. His roles are clear and, as he has long maintained, he will act in accordance with his expected duties. If change comes, it will be due to Parliamentary or "popular" forces. As an example of these forces, one can see the debate caused by the Church of England's decision to bless same-sex marriages. The King was not involved. Instead, he silently looked on as MPs and Peers called for the disestablishment of the state church, the Anglican Communion fractured, and the Church edged closer to civil war.

The King's Ecumenical Nature

"…my heart goes out to all Christians who are being persecuted on account of their faith"— the (then) Prince of Wales, 2014

The King may be an Anglican, but it would be curious to expect him to be solely interested in Anglicanism. After all, he has vowed to protect the Church of Scotland and has close familial links to the Greek Orthodox Church. But his interest is not simply based upon family and duty. Rather, he believes that there is more that unites Christians than divides them.

The Orthodox Churches has been the main beneficiary of the King's theological interest and largesse. The upcoming coronation will demonstrate this, with the inclusion of Greek Orthodox music. Equally, the King has been known to have a particularly deep interest in Transylvania—ironic, given his blood link to Vlad the Impaler. This interest has manifested in him, as Prince of Wales, donating money for the restoration of churches throughout the region. Apart from this, the King is a regular visitor to churches in Serbia and, in a nod to his Greek heritage, has found deep spiritual meaning amongst the monasteries of Mount Athos.

Whilst there are Catholic members of the Royal Family, none are immediate relations to the King. However, the King has demonstrated an impulse to engage with Catholic theology. One reason for this could be his penchant for aesthetics. Unlike the late Queen, the King is more of a High Church Anglican. Catholic liturgy is therefore more comfortable. Indeed, this appreciation may be the strongest since the Stewarts ruled our country. The King has met Pope Saint John Paul II, Pope Benedict XVI, and Pope Francis. These meetings have taken place in the United Kingdom and the Vatican City. Indeed, during a visit to the Vatican in 1985, his ecumenical nature almost caused an incident when he expressed a desire to attend Mass with John Paul II. He was only prevented from doing so when Our late Sovereign Lady personally intervened. Apart from papal visits, the King attended the funeral of John Paul II and the canonisation of Cardinal Newman. Outside of theology, the King has a great interest in environmentalism. His focus in this area is to secure the planet for future generations. In doing so, he is following the guidance of St Francis of Assisi, who, apart from founding the Franciscans, is the patron saint of ecology.

Within the Middle East, the Kind has attempted to create ties with the smaller and – perhaps—more ancient churches. The King has praised Middle Eastern churches for their resilience in the face of inordinate pressures. He has focused much time and attention on the plight of Christians in the region. Indeed, during his 2020 visit to the Holy Land, he attended an ecumenical service at the Church of the Nativity in Bethlehem.

As can be seen, the King desires to foster unity between the branches of Christianity. Though it would be a stretch to say he aims to repair the schisms, he desires tolerance between the branches and an exhortation that Christians should look to what unites them rather than divides them.

The King's Bridge-Building Between Different Religions

"The roots of the faith that we share in the One God, the God of Abraham, give us enduring values' — The (then) Prince of Wales, 1993

The King was a very close friend of the former Chief Rabbi of England, Johnathan Sacks. When he died, the King expressed real and deep despair over the loss. When visiting the Holy Land, the King expressed an appreciation of Judaism, particularly how it is the root religion of the Abrahamic faiths.

Regarding Islam, the King has a clear connection. This is not to do with the King being the alleged direct descendant of Muhammed (by 44 generations), but rather due to his belief that Islam has much to offer the Western world. This does not mean he will prefer Islam to Christianity, but it is a signal that he believes different groups can learn from one another. In particular, the King believes that Islam has much to teach Christianity about having an integrated view of the universe—something he believes Christianity has lost. This is unsurprising, Islamic ritual holds many relics of ancient Christian liturgy.

Cross-referencing between the two faiths, as the King has indicated he would support, could illuminate lost doctrines, proving that (apart from the obvious fundamental differences) the two faiths are not destined to be in a civilisational war. Equally, returning to environmentalism, the King understands that the Quran provides limits to nature's abundance. This accords with his belief that our world is not one of infinite bounty. The King has studied the Quran because he believes that one must closely consider other faiths to truly understand what they are about. Equally, he signs letters to Islamic leaders in Arabic. Whilst only a small gesture, it indicates his deep respect for Islam. Indeed, the King criticised a Danish magazine for publishing cartoon images of the Prophet Muhammed, warning that there should be respect for "what is sacred and precious to others." The King has attempted to use his influence to improve the study of Islam, being the Patron of the Oxford Centre for Islamic Studies. Equally, and perhaps most importantly, he founded Mosaic, an organisation dedicated to providing opportunities to young British Muslims.

Whilst the King has focused on Abrahamic religions, he has time for the other major faiths of the United Kingdom. He has visited many Gurdwaras and Hindu temples. In particular, the King has praised the St John's Centre in Southall, London, which hosts an interfaith community comprising Christians, Muslims, Sikhs, and Hindus. The King also recognised the work the Sikh community has undertaken to promote interfaith relations, highlighting how members of the community rallied during the London Riots of 2011 to stand in front of—and protect—mosques and temples.

The King has an interest in inter-faith dialogue. Similarly, to his ecumenical desires, the King will hope to inculcate tolerance between different faiths and to ask different religions to look beyond what divides them to what, even if small, they can agree upon.

How Will the King Deal With Religion — How Will This Differ From the Past?

"It is the duty to protect the diversity of our country, including by protecting the space for faith itself and its practice through the religions, cultures, traditions, and beliefs to which our hearts and minds direct us as individuals" — from the first speech of HM the King as monarch

Fundamentally, the King is not dogmatic. Whilst a man of deep faith, his spiritual nature and intellectual curiosity mean he will be a bridge-building monarch. As the Defender of the Faith, he will be the head of the Church of England and he will continue to be guided by her message. However, as a "Defender of Faith," his care and attention will spread to all faiths. He will continue to promote inter-faith dialogue and he will continue to emphasise similarities over differences. As when Prince of Wales, he will protect different faiths from whatever threatens them. It will be interesting to see whether he becomes vocal about the increasing tendency for atheists to attack religious faith. Whilst the King was silent about the issue of same-sex marriage within the Church of England—presumably deeming it to be a purely theological issue—he must have noted the anti-religious rhetoric directed at the Church.

In this monarch, guided by spiritualism and intellectual curiosity, we see a break from the past. Whilst Our late Sovereign Lady created room for her increasingly multi-faith subjects, the King will be the first to fully embrace other faiths. This may worry some, but it is a cause for excitement. We have a king who will explore how his role can improve the lot of religion as a whole in this increasingly atheistic society. A king who emphasises ecumenicism in a country where Christians seem to fight ever more bitterly over a rapidly diminishing pool of faithful. A king who, with the firm faith of St. Edward the Confessor, King Henry VI, and Queen Elizabeth the Great, will act as perhaps the most important religious figure within this United Kingdom.

So, on coronation day, let us celebrate this resurgence of an intellectual monarchy unseen since the days of King Charles the Martyr. Let us support the King in his endeavours to promote peace, reconciliation, and faith within society. But, most importantly, let us all join in that immortal anthem and prayer:

*"God Save the King!
Long Live the King!"*

THE FIRST: A FICTIONALIZED ACCOUNT OF HISTORY

Ian Maphet

As he reined his war steed to a stop and regally dismounted, one could be forgiven for thinking here was a man fresh to the battlefield and ready to engage with his enemy, if only one could ignore the blood, mud, and gore caked across his magnificent armor. Constantine's eyes shone with ecstasy and focus as he took in his generals' reports, his relative youth still making its presence known in his eagerness to take in all the details of his victory. His confident assurances from the start of the battle until now had buttressed his generals' own certainty of the outcome of this war and his delight in the outcome was reflected in each one's eyes as they examined the maps and took in the results. Even now, as confident as they had been before the battle, they marveled at winning against all odds.

The sight of the dead, dying, and wounded pierced Constantine's heart, as it always did, but he reminded himself there would be time for mourning later. Word had just reached him that his arch-rival, Maxentius, emperor of Italy and North Africa, had drowned in the Tiber River in his desperate attempt to escape Constantine's army. The temptation to exult in Maxentius' death was near at hand to Constantine, but he resisted and focused on the most important aspect of today's outcome. The sight of the cross in the sky and the words "in this sign thou shalt conquer" (in latin, "in hoc signo vinces") were still fresh in his mind from the day before, and he knew his dream of speaking with the Christ Himself was no mere dream. Jesus had told him that the sign of the cross would lead him into victory, so he had not delayed that morning in making sure that every soldier had the Chi-Rho (a typical sign for Christianity) on his shield before the coming battle. His generals had warned him of the risks of fighting a larger battle force, but Constantine knew beyond any shadow of a doubt that God was with him in that battle and the results proved his faith right.

Since he was a child, his mother had taught him the principles of the Christian faith, something his father tolerated as emperor of the western lands of the Roman Empire. Constantine would never forget the fire in his mother's eyes when speaking of this Jesus who changed the world, and he knew from an early age that despite the cultural taboo he believed that this man was truly the Son of God and the pantheon of gods in the Roman temples were mere fantasies. His faith had guided him when lost, encouraged him when beset by troubles and betrayals, and it now showed him what happened when God guided your hand against a rival superior in numbers and acclaim.

Many had displayed little faith in one as young as him ascending to the throne of emperor when his father had died. Halfway into his third decade of life, politics in the empire were wielded against him without mercy. Those who resisted his ascension the most used the excuse of objecting to one just out of his teen years taking on the mantle of emperor. Looking back now, Constantine didn't think he could blame them, but he still remembered the anger at those who fought against his father's deathbed wishes. Six years later he thanked the Creator God that those who had fought so ferociously against him, in the halls of legislation as well as the battlefield, had given him the opportunity to learn and grow as a leader and commander. Without his father's guidance in Britain, those short, but brutal campaigns with political enemies, and the experience of improving and administering the city of York, he wondered if he would have the political acumen to stand where he did now.

After yesterday's vision and dream, he knew that he had been guided the whole time by a Hand far stronger than his own. He marveled at so many of his mother's encouragements and reminders of the Creator God's faithfulness and guidance being proven true and wondered how she would react when he told her so. He imagined it would be her usual humble acceptance of the truth and a timely piece of scripture. Constantine smiled, thankful that his mother had never faltered in her training of The Way.

While lost in these thoughts, one of his generals cleared his throat and began, "My lord, should we march on Rome?"

"Do not call me lord," Constantine replied. "For there is only one Lord, but yes, let us march to Rome and see how we fare in that city."

The usual process of calling the troops back to formation and arranging the prisoners and taking care of the wounded was immediately begun, but they finally began to make their way the few miles to Rome. "Behold," Flavius, one of his most loyal generals remarked. "The glory of Rome!" Constantine knew what he meant; Rome would be theirs and the wonder of the best soldiers in the world marching in perfect formation would soon belong to Rome. He never tired of the sight of the legions marching forward, their glory reflecting in some small way the glory of the God who had just given them an amazing victory.

Unsure of what to expect with Rome, Constantine made sure his men were ready for anything. He imagined either a resigned acceptance of their faith or a drawn-out fight, but as they approached the city, he realized his preparations were not necessary. Constantine knew Maxentius was less than loved, but he was not expecting the welcome he received when he arrived at that glorious city of myth and legend, Rome. The gates stood open, flags and banners waved, and people crowded the walls and roadways, cheering the hero conqueror Constantine. Tears filled his eyes as he regally acknowledged the cheering crowds. He did not know what was to come, but he knew his God was with him.

He watched the politicians around him as he was crowned emperor of the West. he trusted in His God, but he also knew his God expected him to use the wisdom instilled in him by so many. He made mental notes of those who cheerfully and seemingly genuinely cheered his ascension and those who ground their teeth while trying to look happy about the ceremony. He knew now, no thanks to those who had tried to overthrow or assassinate him before, what to watch out for and how to dodge the traps those who made a show of things would no doubt lay for him.

More importantly, he wanted to move forward with laws he had already instituted in his own regions and was eager to establish in his expanded realm. For nearly 300 years Christians had endured persecutions of all kinds, many inflicted by Roman Law, and Constantine desired to end such persecution. So before almost any other laws were put into place or removed, Constantine made it the law of the West Roman Empire that all religions were to be free to practice their faith, but he also openly promoted Christianity.

This was met with a response that was as expected as it was interesting. A few of the men he originally thought he could rely on objected, on the grounds of often held, but easily disproven myths of atheism and cannibalism (For since the Christians did not worship anyone from the Pantheon, surely they worshiped none at all; and why did they claim to consume the blood and body of the one they also claimed to worship?), but the ones he had already noted as being potential problems displayed their colors.

"How dare you!" One politician screamed at him in the assembly. "This is a cult that has no business being supported by the glory of Rome and her gods! This is a cult that must die!"

"Tell me then," Constantine calmly replied from his throne. "Why has this so-called cult survived almost three centuries of Roman and Jewish efforts to wipe it out?"

The man stuttered for a moment, then regained his composure to point a finger at the sitting emperor. "No one has had the guts to do what was necessary and make sure the gods ruled supreme!"

"So then Nero," Constantine quietly began as he stood and took a step toward the speaker. "Celebrated for using Christians as torches for his lavish parties, did not have the guts to do what was necessary?"

The man began to turn white as Constantine continued, "Tell me why the One this so-called cult worships appeared to me in a dream if it were merely a cult? Tell why this Creator God we had no name for gave me a victory over a superior military might?

"You cannot and thus must experience the fruit of your lack of faith and insight," Constantine gestured to one of his generals. "Make sure this man's titles are removed. Do not physically injure him or his family, but the Empire has no need of such cowards and he is not allowed within these grounds again."

The entire assembly sat in silence as the cries of one of their own faded into the distance, then one by one they turned toward their emperor. Expressing gratitude inside to Jesus, Constantine knew the path had been set; he would be able to pull Christianity out of the brutal cycle of persecution and allow it to really flourish everywhere.

A year later his fellow emperor, Licinius messaged Constantine with questions about his policies toward the followers of The Way. He imagined he had misunderstood what he had heard about Constantine's laws for the West Empire and wanted clarification. Constantine was eager to let Licinius know exactly what his laws and policies regarding Christianity and other religions in the Empire were. Though later it would come to be known as the Edict of Milan, it was merely a letter in which one emperor of an empire explained his established policy to the other emperor and greatly encouraged him to adopt the same policies. Of course, the implication was that the might of his now renowned armies was fully in support of his colleague's following his example.

Licinius took the hint and responded with eager acceptance of Constantine's policies. At least for a year he adopted those policies. Word soon reached the West Empire that Licinius had not only tossed out the toleration of religions and was actively persecuting Christians, but was also conspiring against Constantine himself.

Not long after receiving this news Constantine was looking at the might of his armies drawn up in perfect formation against Licinius' armies. As they went out to meet each other before battle began, Constantine looked up at the sky and for a moment thought he saw a cross outline against the sun. He smiled as he drew up across from Licinius, something that clearly unnerved the other man, and he let Licinius (or rather his representative) lay out terms of surrender. Constantine let the silence linger after the man finished, looking unblinkingly at Licinius. He wondered in his heart if there could be another outcome aside from the one that was clearly unfolding on this field of battle as he rejected the terms of surrender and laid out his own. Licinius, oddly unnerved for one who had held the title of emperor for as long as he had, spat at Constantine in reply, turned his horse and galloped back to his army with his retinue trying to keep up. Constantine sat for a minute, taking in the other army, then let go of the hope that there could be any other outcome.

Soon the screams of men and horses, the agonizing groans of the wounded, and the clash of steel upon steel filled the air. For a moment Constantine wondered if this was one battle the Lord would let him lose, but his attention was soon drawn to his right flank. They were beginning to make progress forward. Slow, painful progress, but progress nonetheless! He watched as the enemy's line shifted back, stretched thin already, then broke, chaos becoming the standard for the men as one army began to turn and run as the other chased them. Constantine watched as the chaos made its way down the entire line, as each successive legion realized what was happening and sounded the retreat or just turned and scrambled to get away from the blood lust that was overtaking Constantine's men.

"There, my emperor," one of his men shouted. "Their standard has fallen; you have won the day!"

Immediately, as his men celebrated their victory, Constantine dismounted and knelt down in the mud. Quickly the men around him realized what was happening and followed suit. Constantine made the sign of the cross on his forehead, his men imitating him in this action, and prayed, "Thank you, oh Lord, for this victory! May you be pleased to grant your servant wisdom in the administration of your great empire to the glory of your name and the good of your Church. Amen."

He rose up, followed by his men, each one watching him closely for his next orders. He took in the battlefield, once again reminding himself that mourning the dead and wounded will have its own time, and noticed Licinius and his retinue being led toward him by a centurion and his men.

"Flavius," he said to the man at his side, never taking his eyes off the sight of the last co-emperor of the Roman Empire being led in shame to accept his judgment. "Make sure that centurion and his men are rewarded generously for their discipline and focus, and that any widows made today among them will never want for sustenance."

"It will be done immediately, my emperor," Flavius replied.

As Licinius was thrown to his knees in front of him, Constantine knew what this meant for him and the Roman Empire. Because of his treason, Licinius would have to be executed, and Constantine would become the sole emperor of the entire Roman Empire, something that had not happened in many years. Eager to press forward for the cause of Christ and to make changes for the betterment of Roman society as a whole, Constantine was also grateful and humbled by the task. He had many dreams and plans for the Empire, but never did he forget the Hands that had given him all of these things.

Constantine would be a huge advocate for the Christian Church, even offering his palace for the use of the Council of Nicea. He would commission bibles (expensive investments at the time), end pagan sacrifices, abortion, and infanticide, seeking justice in all things. What he would never imagine would be that he was merely the first of a long line of emperors and kings who embraced Christ and His Kingdom as preeminent over their own. One thing he could never imagine would be the crowning of a king in a beautiful church building, under the authority of God, in a time in which personal truth and preference trumped all else. One can only imagine his reaction to such a thing!

COMPOSERS AND CORONATIONS

Theodore Harvey

One of Henry Purcell's responsibilities in his role as organist of Westminster Abbey was to write music for the next coronation. King Charles II died in 1685. He had plenty of children; unfortunately, his wife was not the mother of any of them. So his younger brother James, who had already converted to Roman Catholicism, became monarch. This was sort of a surreal moment, because it was the only time that a Roman Catholic monarch was crowned in an Anglican ceremony; he could not take Communion at his own coronation. Purcell wrote this anthem for the coronation, "I Was Glad." Now we're going to hear a slightly more familiar "I Was Glad" later on, but this is the one that Purcell composed for James II in 1685. It is being sung here by the finest exemplar of this tradition in this country, the Saint Thomas Choir of Men and Boys of New York.

Henry Purcell (1659-1695)
I Was Glad

John Scott/The Saint Thomas Choir of Men & Boys with Concert Royal
O Sing Unto the Lord: Sacred Music of Henry Purcell (Saint Thomas Recordings, 2010)

After the so-called "Glorious Revolution," especially when the two Stuart daughters died without heirs and the Hanoverian kings were imported from Germany, the Church of England, while there was nothing to approach the horrors of the Puritans, entered into what might be called a long dry period. Musically, liturgically, there wasn't a lot going on. In fact if you look at church bulletins that print birth and death dates of Anglican composers you'll see that there are a lot of dates from the 1500s and 1600s, a lot of dates from the 1800s and 1900s, but not a lot from the 1700s. This was a century where not as much was happening.

In 1727, the first Hanoverian king, George I, died and was succeeded by his son George II. It perhaps says something about the condition of English music that far and away the most popular composer in England at the time was not English at all, but had been born in Germany: the great George Frideric Handel. Coronations in the eighteenth century were frankly a bit of a mess. This is a wonderful description from this CD. Unfortunately I only have time to play one excerpt from it but again, this is another recording that seems like it was made with this talk tonight in mind: a complete reconstruction of the coronation of King George II. From the jacket we read:

> By the end of September Handel had clearly finished his new compositions. Predictably, with no instructions apparently passed to him (or perhaps they were conveniently ignored), the results come the day of the coronation were delightfully confused. The printed order at times bore little relation to what actually took place. Handel's texts in his own anthems did not match what was printed in the service paper; several anthems were performed at different positions in the service to those officially sanctioned, and some pieces meant to be set to music apparently were not, and vice versa. The actual musical performances too suffered from more than a degree of disorganization. Archbishop Wake, perhaps miffed because he felt Handel had hijacked the order of service, wrote a series of caustic comments in the margin of his own service paper, commencing with 'No Anthem at all Sung... by the Negligence of the Choir of Westminster'; and against Handel's first anthem was marked the terse comment: 'The Anthem all in confusion: All irregular in the Music'. The lack of musical coordination on the day cannot have been helped by the performers' being placed on two specially built platforms on either side of the abbey, their views interrupted by the altar. To make matters worse, five of the ten boys from the Chapel Royal choir had left with broken voices in June and such was the duplication of adult jobs between the two musical establishments that only one singer from the abbey was not accounted for from within the ranks of the Chapel Royal choir.

But today, none of that really matters, because we have one legacy of this coronation that outshines any possible confusion at the time. This is an anthem which I think includes perhaps the most exciting introduction and chorus entrance ever written, the one piece that some of you probably could have predicted I would not dare leave out tonight: Handel's incomparable "Zadok the Priest."

George Frederic Handel (1685-1759)
Zadok the Priest
Robert King/Choir of The King's Consort, The King's Consort
The Coronation of King George II
(Hyperion, 2001)

Coronations did not improve much at the beginning of the nineteenth century when there was a farce of an entirely different kind. King George IV, who succeeded his old, mad father George III in 1820, was estranged from his wife Caroline. Actually I'm not sure if you can be "estranged" from someone that you never liked to begin with. When George saw Caroline for the first time (it was of course an arranged marriage), the first thing he said was, "Pray, get me a glass of brandy." The marriage did not improve. So when it came time to be crowned, Caroline of course considered herself Queen, but George took the rather unusual step of barring Caroline from her own coronation. There was a supremely undignified scene in which Caroline was actually running around to the different doors of Westminster Abbey, banging on them as the guards kept her out. This did not do much for the dignity of her public image.

The death of Queen Victoria inaugurated the twentieth century. When we think of the British Monarchy today, we think of a very high standard in terms of pageantry and ceremonial. However, as I indicated earlier, this has not been consistent through the centuries. It was her son and successor King Edward VII, who loved pageantry, loved putting on a show, who really did a lot to revive and even to a certain extent create this sense of absolutely precise, glorious ceremonial that we take for granted today with the British Monarchy. And this was no less true in the realm of music.

A prominent British musician of the time was the great composer Charles Hubert Hastings Parry. He was the director of the Royal College of Music and a professor at Oxford. His father wanted him to sell insurance, but that didn't go very well. What did go well was writing music, as I think you'll agree. He wrote an anthem originally for Edward VII's coronation in 1902, which has like Handel's "Zadok the Priest" become a permanent fixture at every subsequent coronation. This is of course "I Was Glad," the same text [Psalm 122] as the Purcell we heard earlier, but a much grander and more elaborate setting. You've probably heard this with organ; I wanted to use this particular live recording with orchestra. You may notice that

the balance, which heavily favours the militarily augmented brass, is probably not what you would get on a polished studio recording, but I think that adds an extra dimension of excitement. This is a live royal event in Westminster Abbey, probably very much what this would have sounded like as the Entrance at the coronation of Edward VII in 1902.

Charles Hubert Hastings Parry (1848-1918)
I Was Glad
James O'Donnell/The Choirs of Westminster Abbey and the Chapel Royal Christopher Warren-Green/London Chamber Orchestra
The Royal Wedding: The Official Album (Decca, 2011)

Sadly, Parry, who greatly admired the musical culture of Germany, was devastated by the outbreak of war between the two countries in 1914 and died as a casualty of the flu epidemic of 1918.

Another leading composer of this time was Charles Villiers Stanford (1852-1924), who was born in Dublin but moved to England at the age of ten and studied at Trinity College Cambridge. He later became a professor at both the Royal College of Music and Cambridge. Stanford was known for having a fiery temper which led to some quarrels with his contemporaries, including Parry, but they were always short-lived: when Parry died, Stanford dedicated a Magnificat to his memory. For the coronation of King George V in 1911 (Edward VII having died the previous year), Stanford arranged this Gloria from his Communion Service in B-flat (originally accompanied by organ) for orchestra. Remember that in the 1662 Book of Common Prayer, the Gloria comes at the end of the service, so this sounds very much like a finale. As a cellist I think it exhibits some wonderful writing for orchestra. This Gloria would also be sung at the coronation of George V's granddaughter 42 years later.

Charles Villiers Stanford (1852-1924)
Gloria in Excelsis
Martin Neary/The Choir of
Westminster Abbey
*Music from the Coronation of HM
Queen Elizabeth II* (Cantoris, 1994)

Less than a year after George V died in 1936, his eldest son Edward VIII famously abdicated the throne to marry the twice-divorced American Wallis Simpson. So it fell to Edward's younger brother George VI to lead Britain through World War II, which he did quite heroically. The war took a heavy toll on the King's health, and in 1952 he died at only 56 and was succeeded by his daughter, the late Queen Elizabeth II (1926-2022).

The Queen's coronation on June 2, 1953, arguably represented the pinnacle of twentieth-century Anglican choral music, and certainly constituted a high point of collaboration between Monarchy and Music. We think of coronations as steeped in tradition, and they certainly are, but it's important to remember that they've also long been an opportunity to showcase new music. For this coronation, pieces were commissioned from the most eminent British and Commonwealth composers of the time, including William Harris, George Dyson, Healy Willan, and Ralph Vaughan Williams. I can't play all of them tonight, but I know that my Incarnation choir friends would not let me out of here without including a piece by the one and only Herbert Howells. He wrote this beautiful anthem "Behold, O God Our Defender" for the Introit of the 1953 ceremony; I think the achingly lush sonorities at the beginning, especially with orchestra, are particularly remarkable.

Herbert Howells (1892-1983)
Behold, O God Our Defender
*Music from the Coronation of HM
Queen Elizabeth II*

The youngest composer featured in 1953 was William Walton, who was born in 1902 in Oldham. Walton's career got off to an uncertain start at the age of ten. His parents had seen an advertisement seeking choristers for Christ Church, Oxford and decided William should try out. Unfortunately the night before the audition his father spent the money for the train fare on alcohol at the pub. By the time Louisa Walton managed to borrow money from a grocer and get little William to Oxford, the auditions were over. She convinced the cathedral authorities to hear her son anyway, and since it was already obvious that he was a major talent, they let him in. Walton went on to have quite a distinguished career as a composer, for which he was knighted in 1951. Having already written the march "Crown Imperial" for her father's coronation in 1937, he contributed both another march and this Te Deum for Elizabeth II's coronation. As the final piece of the service prior to the National Anthem, the Te Deum while not neglecting bombast also includes some beautiful quiet moments.

William Walton (1902-1983)
Coronation Te Deum
*Music from the Coronation of HM
Queen Elizabeth II*

Queen Elizabeth II went on to reign for 70 years, becoming one of the most iconic and beloved figures in history. With the accession of her son King Charles III, the world awaits a new British Coronation for the first time in the lives of most of us today. For the May 6 ceremony at Westminster Abbey, the King has commissioned twelve new pieces of music, which will be heard alongside traditional standards such as the Handel and Parry mentioned earlier. While adapted in some ways for the modern world, the Coronation is sure to be a thrilling event for all who witness it, linking our time with a thousand years of history. ❧

A PROTESTANT PILGRIMAGE: PERSONAL REFLECTIONS ON KING WILLIAM OF ORANGE

John Lindsay

Tucked away amongst the mostly rather drab sleeves of my father's record collection was a picture that my childish mind thought was the most beautiful image that had ever been created. Astride a white horse, resplendently attired, his curly locks flowing in the breeze, King William of Orange pointed his sword across the River Boyne to where the forces of tyranny and enemies of liberty were encamped. Their defeat the following day would ensure that justice, harmony, and all that was good would be restored to these Sceptred Isles.

In a culture that eschewed idols, icons, and saints, King Billy fulfilled all of these roles. He was the fairytale prince and king who ensured all of our happily ever afters. The iconic equestrian image, sometimes well painted, other times less so, decorated countless gable ends in Belfast, the city of my birth. In the summer these streets would be festooned with union flags and red white and blue bunting. On the 12th day of July the cream of Belfast's Protestant manhood would put on their best suits and drape radiant orange and purple collarettes around their necks to walk behind flute and drum bands, belting out martial airs to commemorate the anniversary of King Billy's victory at the Boyne. The celebrations have been described as the greatest display of colour and pageantry to be seen anywhere in Western Europe.

I'm an Orangie. Our street was Orange. We weren't Roman Catholics, and at some time back in the day both my mother's and my father's ancestors had attended Protestant churches—my father's family Presbyterian, my mother's Anglican. Elderly Scottish relatives told me stories of Great Aunt Annie Lindsay, who was said to be a crack shot with a Bible aimed at anyone she spotted dozing off in the Kirk. Other more recent relations weren't so fussed about religion but we were still Orangies whether we liked it or not. I must have been aware from an early age that there were other streets that saw things differently. My mother was an economic historian and industrial archaeologist, later a history teacher at a comprehensive school. Her research took her to the old steel foundry on the Catholic Falls Road. Foolishly she told the toddler me not to mention orange when we took the bus there. Of course I spent the entire journey shouting loudly that my favourite colour was orange, and that a very nice colour it was too. My mother did not record the reaction of the other passengers. I hope that their empathy for a mother dealing with an annoying little brat trumped their disapproval of our being of the other sort.

We moved away from Belfast in 1966, while I was still very young. A few years afterwards, Belfast descended into a violent sectarian conflict known, with euphemistic understatement, as "the Troubles." History lessons at primary school in our new home in North Wales told us of the greatness of the British Empire, that the Welsh were better than the English but that nonetheless Britain was the best, a guiding light to the rest of the world. King Billy barely featured in this story. We were told that something glorious happened in 1688, that it should be easy to remember, because it happened a century after the Spanish Armada, when a Welsh dynasty had been on the throne. William and Mary were the last joint monarchs during the slightly dull period after the Tudors and Stuarts but before the heroic age of pirates and the glorious war against that rotter Napoleon.

E.C. Fuller's parody on the history teaching of the period, *1066 and All That* describes his reign thus:

"WILLIAMANMARY (sic) for some reason was known as the Orange in their own country of Holland, and were popular as King of England because the people naturally believed it was descended from Nell Glynn. It was on the whole a good king and one of their first Acts was the Toleration Act, though afterwards it went back on this and they decided that they could not tolerate the Scots…

… Meanwhile the Orange increased its popularity and showed themselves to be a very strong King by its ingenious answer to the Irish question; this consisted in the Battle of the Boyne and a very strong treaty which followed it, stating that (a) that all the Irish Roman Catholics who liked could be transported to France, (b) that all the rest who liked could be put to the sword, (c) that Northern Ireland should be planted with Blood Orangemen.

These Blood Orangemen are still there; they are of course all descendants of Nell Glyn and are extremely fierce and industrial and so loyal that they are always ready to start a loyal rebellion to the Glory of God and the Orange. All of which shows that the Orange was a Good Thing, as well as being a good King. After the treaty the Irish who remained were made to go live in a bog and think of a New Question."

The parody wasn't that different from what we were taught, the main difference being that it was more entertaining.

Fashions in history teaching changed as I entered my teenage years in the 1970s. Patriotism fell out of vogue. Empire and imperialism became dirty words, and the narrative in the teaching about the British Empire switched from its philanthropic mission to an almost exclusive focus on its evils. If William of Orange manages a mention in today's history textbooks it may relate to his takeover of the Royal African Company founded by his father in law and predecessor on the throne, and the millions that it made from the trans-Atlantic slave trade—and it is of course right that those horrors are not forgotten.

Punk rock happened. I embraced it and its rejection of deference. When I moved back to Northern Ireland at the age of twenty in 1984, and started to meet people from the Catholic community and listen to their take on the events that they'd lived through, the heroes of my childhood came out in a very different light.

Was it possible that we were the bad guys?

I don't think that we are, because that's not the way that history works. It's more complicated than that.

Who then was the real King William of Orange, and what is the legacy, both of the man himself, and the myths that have grown up around him?

William was a prince from the day of his birth (November 4, 1650). His father, also William, died a week before he was born. The princely title passed to him as his only son and heir. His grandfather, William the Silent (also William of Orange) had been a leader in the wars that freed the United Provinces of the Netherlands from Spanish Hapsburg rule. He was baptised and raised a Protestant within the Calvinistic tradition, closer in beliefs and values to Scottish Presbyterianism than to the Episcopalianism of the Church of England to which he formally converted when he took the English throne.

William was never a king in Holland—which, formally at least, remained a loosely confederated republic until the nineteenth century. Dutch royalist enthusiasm for the colour orange comes from common roots, but the Dutch kings called William don't include our King Billy. Some years ago, with little understanding of this, and presuming that the ubiquitous banners reading "Wij houden van Oranje" (We love Orange) meant that they were kindred spirits, I pressed an Amsterdam tour guide on the legacy of our King William there. His reply was not what I expected. He didn't want to talk about King Billy, instead he told me about the "Rampjaar" (disaster year), the terrible events that led indirectly to William of Orange becoming Stadtholder of the United Provinces of the Netherlands in 1672.

The period 1588 to 1672, is sometimes referred to as the Dutch Golden Era. The country prospered, as Calvinistic countries seem wont to do. It was also a haven for toleration and sanctuary for Protestant, Jewish, and free-thinking refugees. The arts flourished, as did the sciences. Ideological rivalry led to numerous conflicts with their absolutist and Catholic French neighbours. Economic rivalry to wars with England. In 1672 the two foes joined forces and invaded. The country was laid waste to. The nation previously famed for its practicality and reasonableness played host to the lynching and partial cannibalisation of their Stadtholder (captain general). William of Orange was installed as stadtholder in his place and tasked with picking up the pieces.

My hero's coming to power in his native land marked, it would seem, not the apogee, but epitaph of a golden age.

The nation previously famed for its practicality and reasonableness played host to the lynching and partial cannibalisation of their Stadtholder ...

The Rampjaar demonstrated the fragility of the Republic to outside tyrannies, most manifest at that time in the absolutist regime of Louis XIV in France. William's response to this was a pragmatic one. He was a shrewd diplomat. As well as firming up links with natural allies—the Swedes, the Danes, and the German Protestant Principalities—he understood that his enemies' enemies were his friends.

One way in which he safeguarded such alliances was through his marriage to Mary, the niece of his erstwhile enemy Charles II, the King of England. The marriage would prove even more serendipitous after Mary's father succeeded his brother on the English throne. It was not a love match but it's said to have been characterised by very genuine affection. He took mistresses. That was the norm amongst European royalty. His wife was said to have been more concerned about the peril this placed on his immortal soul than by any feeling of betrayal.

There has been a lot of speculation that William may have been an active bisexual. Perhaps he was—in his later life he certainly had close bonds with male companions. It's not a question that we're ever likely to get a definitive answer to after such a long passage of time. To his credit William himself is said to have taken a good humoured approach when the rumours were put to him. It was no one else's business. It's sometimes thrown at current members of the Orange Order (who are in reality more of a religious organisation with political dimensions than a fan club for the late monarch) by their detractors. Does it matter? Almost certainly not.

Another part of William's alliance building that is sometimes thrown at William's supporters as though it exposes a fatal flaw in their ideology are the good relations that William built with the Vatican. On the face of it, it

certainly seems surprising. The Dutch republic's values of religious toleration and accountable government rested to a large extent on its Calvinist traditions. The very idea of a Pope is anathema to Calvinists, an idolatrous inversion of the priesthood of all believers. When looked at more closely the alliance was extremely expedient and greatly to the advantage and credit of both parties. Pope Innocent XI was a cultured and educated man. Educated by the Jesuits, and trained in civil law, he had worked with providing relief to plague victims prior to his election to the papacy. As Pope he campaigned against nepotism in the Catholic Church and for the personal morality and behaviour of priests to be brought in line with Christian teachings. He was also financially astute, lowering taxes but still managing to produce a surfeit in the budget of the Papal States.

Perhaps these character traits were a factor in his coming into conflict with the extravagant Louis XIV of France. Louis's absolutism also led him to exercise greater control over the Catholic Church in France, but the real breaking point came when Louis XIV moved militarily against the Papal States in Avignon. When James II of England began to establish closer ties with Louis XIV, Pope Innocent discreetly began to support the Protestant William against the two Roman Catholic monarchs.

Absolutism reached a new low in 1685, the year of James II/VII's coronation, when Louis of France revoked the Edict of Nantes, the law that had brought an end to the French Wars of Religion almost a century earlier, and brought a measure of religious toleration and secularism to French government and society. After the revocation, it became illegal to be a Protestant in France. In England, King James made what looked at first glance to be a move in the opposite direction, dismissing Parliament to force through a "Declaration of Indulgence" supposedly to remove restrictions on Roman Catholics and dissenting Protestants, closing the Scottish Parliament to enforce a similar measure there a year later. He began to replace officials with Roman Catholic favourites. The "indulgence" was a facade. Scottish Covenanters were rounded up, imprisoned, and executed en masse.

In England the crunch came when Bishops who refused to accede to his usurpation of Parliament and swear allegiance to the king and his successors were taken to the Tower of London and charged with treason. News that James's second wife had given birth to a son (or according to some accounts a male child had been smuggled into her bedchamber in a warming pan) moving Mary and her sister Anne further down the line of succession, heightened fears that the slide into absolutist tyranny might be irreversible.

Almost the entire country turned against the King. Delegates of the prorogued Parliament went to the Hague begging William to intervene, telling him that he would be met with a heroes' welcome if he came to England with an army behind him to take the throne.

William considered his options. He studied the broader international situation, particularly the intentions of the French regime. Then, on November 4, 1688, his 38th birthday, he set sail for England, landing in Torbay in Devon to avoid a fleet that might still have been loyal to James in London, William marched towards London meeting little to no resistance.

Outflanked, James fled to seek sanctuary with his ally, the French despot. Parliament met and declared that James's desertion constituted an abdication, and invited William and his wife to take the throne in his stead. With barely a shot fired, for England

at least, the Glorious Revolution had been won. Britain was changed utterly. Never again would a King, of England or of Scotland, be able to rule without the consent of Parliament. Over time, as the franchise was extended to all of the Crown's subjects, this would mean that a sovereign could only reign by the consent of citizens. British democracy, the constitutional monarchy, was born.

It would be tempting to close this story on this note, but of course it doesn't end there. There was some resistance to William's accession in Scotland than in England, especially in the largely Roman Catholic Highlands. Jacobite soldiers had some success at the Battle of Killiecrankie (the name of that battle for some reason used to prompt giggling amongst my mother's students in 1970s Llandudno) but were halted by Williamite forces at Dunkeld. I've visited Dunkeld to pay homage to this victory with Scottish members of the Orange Order. The legacy of this Highland resistance lived on in infamy later, when King William signed off the order that led to the massacre of members of the McDonald clan by members of the Campbell clan at Glencoe. It was perhaps the one most indisputably shameful act of his reign.

Then there is the other island. An island where, as I said at the start, William's memory is still very much alive. Ireland had its own bloody history of grudges and sacrifice—invasion, settlement, massacres of settlers and massacres in reprisal. It suited James and his French backers to exploit these to seek support from his coreligionists. James sailed to Kinsale in the South of Ireland to raise an army. James is not remembered fondly in Catholic Ireland. He was nicknamed Séamas an Chaca (James the Sh-t).

William came to Carrickfergus in the North to meet him. Irish Catholics, the majority of the island's people, had good cause to rally behind James. Protestants had perhaps better cause to believe that their survival depended on the success of William.

I'll not reprise the details of the war in Ireland that followed. There was real heroism on the part of the besieged citizens of Londonderry, who held out, half starving against a Jacobite army (James himself came to the city walls to taunt them) for 105 days before British ships broke through the River Foyle to come to their relief). Had they not done so then the path might have lain open for James to sail to Scotland and try to retake the throne.

As a member of the Apprentice Boys of Derry, a fraternity established to remember the young apprentices who closed the city's gates against King James's soldiers at the beginning of the siege, I'm proud to wear a crimson collarette (the colour of the flag that flew above the besieged city) to remember those brave defenders of what is now my home city when we parade every December and August to mark the anniversaries of the beginning and ending of that siege.

William led his troops from the front to meet King James and his men at the Boyne— the image on my father's record sleeve and on countless walls across Northern Ireland. He won. Religious toleration of the kind that William genuinely believed in did not follow, but I'll let others take up that tale.

William went on to reign for another 12 years. His Calvinistic values may, some argue, have made Britain a more tolerant country than she was before. He spent much of his reign abroad, involved in continental wars. His absence may have helped to reinforce the primacy of Parliament over the Crown. Parliament governed and made laws. The King reigned.

While her husband was away, Queen Mary was said by those who met her to be an attentive and insightful sovereign, listening to the concerns, and occasionally offering advice to her government. In 1694 she fell ill with smallpox and died. Before her death she sent the members of her household who had escaped the contagion away for their own protection. When she died later that year, King William was said to be genuinely wracked with grief. William himself died in 1702, as the result of a riding accident, when the horse upon which he was riding caught its hoof in a molehill. Jacobite supporters in Scotland are said to raise a toast to the "gentleman in the velvet jacket" in commemoration of this happenstance. As with snakes and weasels, we do not have native moles in Ireland.

That's my take on King Billy then. It's an account by a supporter, so it isn't impartial, but I have tried to be fair.

Whatever faith you may follow, and whatever your politics—and you should of course always be free to follow your conscience in such matters—may I invite you to raise a toast to the glorious memory of King Billy.

The Coronation of Queen Victoria in
Westminster Abbey, 28 June 1838
by George Hayter, 1839

CAKE IS BETTER

Hannah Skipper

(in memory of Marie Antoinette)

The howling masses shall not go hungry.
Let them eat cake.
Cake is better.
They call for bread; whining in the streets for pumpernickel, sourdough, and rye.
Of course, they do; they're just ignorant rabble.
Needing a royal hand like mine to show them the best way.
Bread may be nutritious, but cake is delicious.
Don't they know? How could they not?
Don't their personal chefs feed them the right way?
Let them eat cake.
Cake is better.
Spread the frosting, layer on the sprinkles, lick the icing off the side.
Let them eat cake.
Cake is better.
They say that bread and water are for surviving.
I say cake is for thriving.
Besides, what else would I serve my guests?
Please don't let the people ruin my party.
Please send that loud complaining mob away.
Let them eat cake.
Cake is better.
Why are the people railing on the streets now?
They have no right to agitate against the king and I.
We only want what's best for them.
That's always been our goal.
What did the Estates eat at their meeting anyways?
Didn't they have their fill at that famous tennis match?
Let them eat cake.
Cake is better.
Oh, how I long to cut just one more piece.
There's so much slicing going on these days.
Why can't we all just eat a little more?
My party simply can't end this way.
Let them eat cake.
Cake is better.

Artwork: *Still Life with Bread and Sweetmeats*
by Georg Flegel, ca. 1633 – 1636

THOUGHTS ON THE CORONATION

Henry Hill

On Friday, March 3, 2023, the sacred Chrism oil which will be used to anoint King Charles III at his coronation was consecrated at the Church of the Holy Sepulchre in Jerusalem. As illustrations of what makes the British monarchy special go, it was hard to beat.

The photographs tweeted by the Royal Family show the Patriarch of Jerusalem, alongside the Anglican archbishop, engaging in a ritual which hasn't been performed at all since the late Queen Elizabeth was crowned in 1953, and will *deo volente* not be performed again for many years yet.

To some, it will doubtless seem absurd. The pomp and pageantry that accompanies the monarchy is often criticised, not only by explicit republicans but those who hold what we might call republican attitudes. Even if the head of state is not elected, ought not the office be more modern? More relevant to life in Britain today?

The coronation has become a locus for such complaints. Not only has the ritual come under predictable attack, but the cost—estimated at some £50 million (about $60.2 million)—denounced as inappropriate given the cost-of-living crisis facing many of His Majesty's subjects as spiralling energy costs and our broken housing market squeeze the incomes of working people.

Yet both these arguments entirely miss the point of monarchy, especially a constitutional monarchy in a modern, democratic state. The splendour is the point.

The financial cost is, in the grand scheme of things, trivial. Even if the entire event were scrapped entirely, a few tens of millions is a drop in the ocean relative to the vast expenditure of the British state.

It is also great value for money. As mentioned above, we haven't had a coronation since 1953. Contrast this with a republic which must stage an inauguration every four or eight years. The Biden Inauguration Committee reportedly raised $61.8 million—and that was just the most recent presidential handover!

Artwork: *King George III in coronation robes* by Allan Ramsay, ca. 1765

Yes, of course the coronation could be staged more cheaply. Half of the face cost of it is security costs, but presumably the military and police could throw up their ring of steel around a registry office, or similarly spartan venue, wherein the King and Archbishop of Canterbury could get the whole thing done and dusted in half an hour.

At a stroke, £25 million or so saved for the public purse! That's enough to run the National Health Service for, er, about three hours.

But to approach the question as an accountant is to risk, as was sometimes said of Margaret Thatcher, seeing the price of something but not the value of it. For the truth is that the Crown's subjects would not only gain very little from disenchanting the monarchy, but they would lose much.

There is no alternative stock of magic in the British constitution. The royal family is at the centre of all our pageantry, not just rarities such as coronations but more regular events such as the state opening of Parliament and the Trooping of the Colour.

A big advantage of this is that such events can thus—with the obvious but relatively minor exception of republicans–be enjoyed equally by everyone, because at the centre of them is a nonpartisan individual rather than a politician.

By contrast, even in a country as steeped in barely-concealed monarchical sentiment as France, the great ceremonies of the state must necessarily, by dint of their republican constitution, have at their heart a political figure, for whom many citizens did not vote and whose policies many may bitterly oppose.

This is one factor which has allowed royal occasions to becoming unifying moments, time stamps in the memories of the British people—a chance to remember where you where when, and who you were with.

Another is that unlike the mechanical timetable of politics, with its regular elections, the pattern of royal occasions is an irregular, organic and very human one, marked by births, weddings, funerals, and jubilees. The Royal Family is a family, the monarch a human being, and it is that human element which has helped the House of Windsor maintain that enduring connection with its subjects that so baffles the rationalists and the modernisers.

People like pageantry, they cherish beauty, they remember spectacle. That's why so many republics invest so heavily in pageantry, for all that British republicans seem to forget it. The splendour of monarchy plays into these strengths, and in a manner that if anything has far less capacity for malicious misuse than the inherently political deployment of national iconography a republic entails.

Besides which, the last thing people need is for the monarchy to reflect their day-to-day lives—they encounter the everyday. The pomp and circumstance of the Crown is a sprinkling of national magic.

Asset-strip the Crown, and we would soon find only that our count of enchanted objects—kings and queens, princes and princesses, coronations and jubilees—had diminished, and by more than one.

We would also lose an irreplaceable connection to the history of one of the most ancient constitutions on Earth. The preparations in Jerusalem is just a particularly vivid example of the deeper truth that participation in shared ritual is a way of building a connection with our ancestors, and of giving our descendants the same opportunity for a moment of common feeling with our own day.

As British society has grown more diverse, and the rise of the Internet has broken the oligopolies of traditional media, such shared moments are rarer than they used to be. We can no longer, as our ancestors might, assume our fellow citizens have served in the Armed Forces, or attended church, or read certain books, or learned in school a common narrative about our country.

That makes those instances that remain the more precious, and with occasional exceptions such as hosting the Olympics in 2012, the monarchy is the custodian of nearly all of them. And in turn we, the people, are the custodians of the monarchy and our other ancient institutions. It is not just great folly but great vanity to cast away this inheritance, and deny it to future generations, by demanding that the United Kingdom reflect in every particular our fleeting image of what modernity looks like.

It's true that the sovereign no longer rules over us, and that the nobility in their ermine are no longer the great power brokers they were when their forefathers fought or bought their way to the table however many centuries ago. Nor is today's Britain the overwhelmingly Anglican nation that it was even a generation ago.

Yet that doesn't mean that those institutions aren't important, as reminders of from whence we have come and thus, inevitably if only in part, of who

we are. Inevitably, George Orwell put it best when he wrote in *The Lion and the Unicorn*:

> *"What can the England of 1940 have in common with the England of 1840? But then, what have you in common with the child of five whose photograph your mother keeps on the mantelpiece? Nothing, except that you happen to be the same person."*

On Saturday, May 6, 2023, I will join tens of millions of my fellow Britons, tens of millions more of his subjects in the Commonwealth realms, and likely hundreds of millions of people around the world to watch the coronation of Charles III. In my whole life, it is unlikely I will share such a moment with that many people more than a handful of times.

Alongside the vast majority of them, I will repeat what Winston Churchill called "the prayer and the anthem": God Save the King. And if you think it matters whether or not those who say it believe in the Archbishop of Canterbury's God, or any, you have again missed the point.

ROYAL MAUNDY

Jason Plessas

"Mandatum novum do vobis."

The King hears the words, as does every other being in the great Cathedral. They apply to all, but—tonight—to him in particular.

Sure enough, the King is shortly presented with a humble bowl of water. He gazes into its shallow dullness, then glances over at the most contemptible array of subjects gathered from this far-flung outpost of the Kingdom. From their matted hair, to their decrepit, weather-beaten features, down along the miserable sacks passing for clothing and finally to the bare, loathsome, ulcerous appendages he can just about recognise as feet...

He stifles a shudder. *Can this be right? Perhaps this is all a mistake. I am God's anointed... Lord, let this bowl pass from my...*

No. It is right. It is commanded. *Mandated.*

"I give you a new commandment."

King Edward—in his most honest moments—would concede he had not been the best student of the Holy Scripture, or even the weight of his own position in the Great Chain of Being. At his studies, he had been easily distractible...

But in his faith he was sincere, and this was not complicated: *"Mandatum novum do vobis."*

Love one another.

And so Edward II—King of England; Duke of Aquitaine; Prince of Wales; Lord of Ireland—took up his bowl, knelt before the abject creatures assembled, and one by one, poured water over their feet.

Edward was practising *pedilavium*—literally "foot-washing." It was he who introduced this act of *de imitatione Christi* to the annual Royal Maundy service in Rochester Cathedral during his tumultuous reign.

The lineage of Royal Maundy can be traced at least back to 600, and it is the most unlikely monarch of John who is first recorded as distributing Maundy Money—alms to needy subjects—at Knaresborough Cathedral in 1210, thus first identifying the ideal of Christian service as also a specifically kingly one. But with the practice of pedilavium, it was his tortured, pious great-grandson who truly embodied it.

And so it would continue. Like any tradition, Royal Maundy grew with time, accruing ever more subtraditions as various monarchs distinguished themselves by ever-more grandiose displays of humility. John's issuing of 13 pence

Artwork: *Christ Washing the Disciples' Feet* by Benvenuto Tisi, ca. 1520s

each to 13 men in 1213 had by 1363 sprawled into Edward III's distribution of 50 pence each to 50 commoners, marking his own age of that year. A decree by Henry IV later made the monarch's age the fixed determinant of the amount given.

Royal consorts also became known devotees of Maundy almsgiving, to the extent that Catherine of Aragon had to plead permission from her divorced husband that she might continue to "keep her Maundy"; only in 1536—five years after their separation—did he relent. Understandably then, Catherine's daughter Mary became the monarch most renowned for her adherence to Royal Maundy. The devout 41-year-old Catholic performed pedilavium to forty-one common women "while ever on her knees," plus donating the customary 41 pence to each along with food and clothing, including a gown of her own to a woman said to be the poorest. Mary's half-sister Elizabeth was also a noted practitioner, though she opted for neat purses containing the Maundy Money to avoid unseemly graspings and tearings that had sometimes resulted from gifting royal garb.

It was in the Stuart era that the Royal Maundy traditions started to fray. Charles I was an infrequent attendee and of course everything went fine for him. His son Charles II for some reason thought it wise to steadfastly counteract this, even making sure to attend during the Great Plague year of 1665. The end for royal pedilavium was nigh, however; the last king to have practised it was his brother James II in 1685.

The reign of William and Mary presented an opportunity for paupers of both sexes to receive alms, as traditionally the beneficiaries were of the same sex as the Sovereign. From the reign of George I (1714-27), an equal number of men and women received donations, the number of each sex corresponding to the age of the King. So, in 1720, when George was 60, 60 men and 60 women each received 60 pence. (This would be economically interesting today in our times of perennially elder monarchs and 94 gender identities...)

The other significant thing about George's Maundy practice was his absence; as notoriously German as he was disinterested in his island kingdom, the first Georgian king's Maundy duties were deputised to the Lord High Almoner or even (ouch...) *Sub*-Almoner. The only Hanoverian who distinguishes himself here is William IV who kindly ensured that money—by that time, 30 shillings—was indeed given rather than foodstuffs worth that amount, as some naïve recipients had been found selling their gifts for less than their value. But it was not until the Second Georgian era that another monarch attended, and then only once—George V in 1932 (though less senior royals including Royal Consorts had done so).

In fact, the last recorded monarchical attendance had been 1698, four years before the death of William III due to a riding accident. Paining as may be for this loyal supporter of the 1688 Settlement to admit, it does seem that the fulsomeness of Royal Maundy was a casualty of the "Protestantization" of the monarchy. While one might whiggishly suggest that Parliamentary Sovereignty had negated any strict need, it's clear that something special was lost.

Not forever though. Among the many distinctions of our much-mourned late Queen Elizabeth was her wholehearted revival of Maundy Money. Beginning in 1954, she attended Royal Maundy and presented—by that time, purely symbolic—alms to pensioners recognised by their parish churches for charity work. With characteristic diligence, she missed the service only four times prior to the 2020-21 pandemic, two of which she was represented by her mother. She also ensured geography would be no barrier to participation, decreeing that the ceremony not take place in London more than once in ten years; an act of levelling up before Dominic Cummings and Boris Johnson had ever been heard of. Leicester became the last Anglican Cathedral in England to host Royal Maundy in 2017. Her dedication to Maundy affirmed it as "part of the modern monarch's armoury," as Revd Dr. William Whyte put it.

So then, what of *regiis pedilavium*? Would that be so wacky in today's cynical world? Its revival would be a taller order; if Her Late Majesty delivered resuscitation to Maundy Money, royal pedilavium would require full-blown resurrection.

Nonetheless, in no particular order, a case for its return:

Demonstrate the Christian ideal of the Servant King

Church historian Bruce L. Shelley identified Christianity as "the only major religion to have as its central event the humiliation of its god." If King Charles III wants to walk in the path of that God—and I have every confidence that he does—then what better way than kneeling before the least of his brothers—and sisters? Let's not forget another religious leader's success in re-centring pedilavium: "This is a symbol, it is a sign—washing your feet means I am at your service," Pope Francis told 12 convicts in his first Maundy Mass as Pontiff in 2013.

Inculcate the Next Generation

Full disclosure, this is a hobby-horse of your writer's, who spent the locked-down Maundy Thursday of 2020 blogging an embittered screed demanding lesser royals take a good course in "doing unto the least." This would surely help weed out any entitled misconceptions that modern monarchy is about privilege before it is about service. Yes, recent iterations have been cut off and increasingly satirised out of the public eye, but prevention is better than cure. Henry III ensured all his children accompanied him for his Maundy duties. Wouldn't that be more preemptive than relying on *South Park* and *Prince Andrew: the Musical* to clean up our mess?

Undercut the Identitarian-Left

We are never quite out of the republican woods, and the monarchy has survived partly through hypervigilance in narrative warfare. No, they'll never convince everyone, but the little things royals do can accumulatively resonate. Consider the impact of the Firm's "secret weapon," the royal walkabout for instance. A YouGov survey of 2017 suggested up to a third of the British population had seen the Queen in real space: "That 20 million undergoes a compounding effect because, when you meet the world's most famous woman, you want to share the experience," argued Colin Brazier. Having your feet washed by a senior royal would certainly be a more niche ripple effect than handshakes on the Court Circular, but a profound one in its way. One thing I would not have considered in early 2020 was the impact it could have on Critical Race Theory-driven narratives. The royals can say little-to-nothing for or against the outlandish demands for "reparations" from baiting Caribbean politicians, but wouldn't Prince William and Princess Catherine kneeling before ex-convicts in St. John's Cathedral, Antigua, or Zara and Mike Tindall before OAPs in St. George's Cathedral, the Windward Islands send a message about who's really checking their privilege?

Just a thought. ❧

- Note: All credit for Royal Maundy research goes to Brian Robinson, "The Royal Maundy," (1977), Virginia Cole, "Ritual charity and royal children in thirteenth century England," (2002) and Revd. William Whyte (2010) https://www.churchtimes.co.uk/articles/2010/2-april/features/keepers-of-the-queen-s-purse
- Colin Brazier on royal walkabout (2021): https://www.spectator.co.uk/article/the-queen-has-a-secret-weapon-in-the-war-of-the-waleses/
- And for those with nothing better to do, Jason Plessas (2020): https://occidentalpartridge.blogspot.com/2020/04/maundy-monarchy-and-pedalavium.html

THE KING'S GOOD SERVANT

Leah Fisher

King Henry VIII pressed his palms firmly on the wide stone sill of the open window and stared out longingly. Outside, some of the women walked far below him, in the garden not yet in bloom. The light breeze blew, shifting his auburn hair and causing the white fur of his hat to dance as though it was nervous. He was sure that the warmth and colors of springtime would soon come to comfort him after what had proven to be a dreadfully long winter, but...

"You did summon me," his friend's voice cast hollowly behind him.

"Good Lord High Chancellor..." the king addressed him, removing his hat and casting it down from the window. He watched it fall to the earth. "I'd wager someone will fetch it for me. What do you think?"

"I suspect that there is not a man in England who would fail to return it," his friend assured.

"Yes, I suppose you're right." The king frowned and turned slowly to his friend. "What say you, Thomas? Does God ever throw hats?"

"I think my lord may find that in the case of our Lord, it is we who throw our crowns before Him," the chancellor replied with even tone and the corner of his mouth turned upwards.

The king laughed. "You always have the answer for me, Thomas, always so quick with the response!"

He took a few short steps back towards his desk and bit his lip. Then, turning suddenly on his heel back to his companion, he said, "I'll tell you why I throw my hat: I throw my hat, because I need to know someone will fetch it. I like the thing, but it's a terrible burden on my head. Sometimes, I want to cast it all away; then I could forget about my duty and my honor along with it. I could be free to do as I like, but..."

He caught a glimpse of his friend's stare, pointed and warning, and a sudden chill ran through him. "Well, as you said, someone will fetch it." He paused. "I sometimes wish they wouldn't."

"And yet they will," his friend replied. "They will precisely because of that duty and that honor from which you wish to flee, because God has made you king over England."

"Ah, yes! And does it please Him to frustrate me?" Henry shot back, his voice brimming with discontent. "How shall a king have no heir? How shall I have no son to follow me? A decade of marriage to a worthy woman has produced for me nothing but grief! And where is God to bless the throne He has given?"

"I never thought of what a curse it is to have such a beloved wife and a daughter who adores you," Thomas stated, smiling. "That's a cross which I bear, also, with my Meg. But she and my wife do the heart so good that I wonder...is it really so great of a burden?"

The king sighed. "The love that I once had is waning, and with what gratitude should I rejoice in the shortcomings of my Queen, that she has failed in her duty, as I have? I have broad shoulders, Thomas, but they cannot carry the weight of the world upon them!"

"Then give it to God!" Thomas insisted. "Throw your crown before Him. He never meant for you to bear the weight of it alone, anyway."

Henry shook his head. "You'll tell me to go back to Catherine next and to forget this thing with Anne, but I promise it's no good." He turned back to the window and admired the beauty of the woman who walked with such divine grace in the midst of the barren garden. "My heart is set on something else."

"Are you certain it is your truest heart and not your eyes that wander?" Thomas answered boldly. "For a man ought to pledge his heart but once, and by his word he is bound. How can another soul trust you when the one to whom yours cleaves is held in such derision by you? As king, you have pledged yourself to this people as surely as you have your wife. Or would you divorce them, also?"

"Why are you the voice of my conscience?" Henry lamented. "Can you not leave me here in peace? Will you not let me reason? Like Clement, you will not yield. Catherine is my brother's wife! Must I shout it? I will repent of my love for her, and not for Anne!"

"No, this isn't right! You know this isn't right." Thomas shook his head and approached his monarch, speaking with a pleading expression. "Of what then shall you repent? Of your fidelity, rather than your lust? How shall God accept such a fool hearted repentance? How shall England prosper by your rule apart from the blessing of God?"

For a moment, the king's eyes met his friend's, but quickly turned away, unwilling to face him. "Clement isn't any more God than I am," he muttered. "Why should the Church of Rome command the Church of England?"

Thomas' hands closed into loose fists. For the first time, he had become angry. "The Church of Christ is not divided," he stated dryly.

The king glanced back at his friend. His body was unusually rigid, and his eyes lacked the warmth to which the king was so accustomed. But this time the king met his gaze and did not shy away from it. "And yet, somehow we continue to arrest all those bloody heretics."

"And would you join them in transgression? Your office cannot save you from the wrath of God. A king is not above His Law," his chancellor warned.

It was then that a member of the guard stepped into the doorway. Dressed in full royal uniform with pike in hand, he bowed before his king. "I beg your pardon, my lord," the man said, "but I believe you dropped this."

He held up the king's hat.

"Ah, my hat!" Henry proclaimed in triumph, gesturing towards the door. "You see, Thomas? It always comes back. Why don't you fetch it for me?"

In silent obedience to his monarch, Thomas did as the king asked, thanking the guardsman at the door with sincerity of speech before returning the hat to its wearer. Gleefully, the king took it from him and placed it back atop his head again, as though it was the closing point of some great argument.

"Well, what say you now?" the king challenged. "Do you fancy yourself a traitor?"

"A traitor?" Thomas shook his head, and his countenance changed. The kindness returned to his eyes along with a deep sadness, and a pained expression marked his pale features. "No. I am the king's good servant; but God's first."

SINS OF THE FATHER

Isabella Summitt

Henry V followed the solemn procession. It was the second funeral he had attended in the past two months. Funerary rights were becoming a regular routine in his kingly duties, and he had stayed strictly solemn to accommodate them. He knew how to keep pace with the priest and the pallbearers behind the coffin, taking a step every time the incense shakers swung back and forth. The smoke swirled like ghosts among the drapes and black vestments worn by the deacons. The bells were ringing at slow intervals up in the tower at the abbey. They called all the citizens of London to come and view the procession. A very sparse crowd had answered them and gathered by the side of the road, held back by the soldiers. Their eyes followed the living king, not the coffin of the dead one. Henry kept his eyes low, and his expression neutral, but he couldn't help but wonder what they thought of this spectacle.

Richard II had been dead for over ten years, so the coffin was closed. Their procession entered the abbey through the main gate at the west side. The large doors swung wide open to welcome Richard to the vault that was the final resting place of so many other English kings. The choir began chanting Dies Irae when they passed the arcanex, their voices reverberating off the ancient stone walls. They descended into the vault beneath the shrine of Saint Edward. The candle flames bobbed up and down with every stone step.

They came down into a latticed area, the lavish tomb where Richard's first wife and true love had been years before buried. Richard had planned for the two of them to be buried together, but then he had also planned to live out the rest of his days as the King of England. The pallbearers carefully lifted the coffin over the stone niche prepared for it, and then laid the bronze effigy lid over it. It fell into place with a final resounding thud. The priest knelt in prayer, and Henry followed suit.

"In nomine patris, et filii, et spiritui sancti…"

What, did he think he could bribe God by doing this? It was a bit late to give the crown back to Richard. Henry tried to shake that thought out of his head as he prayed for the repose of the deposed Richard II. Thank God Henry's father had requested to be

Artwork: *King Henry V* by unknown artist, 16th century

buried at Canterbury instead of here, putting him next to the liege he had betrayed would not have pleased his soul. Yet, if his father had not taken up arms against him and become Henry IV, Bolingbroke the Usurper, Henry would not be here now, the king and lord of this storied isle.

"*Requiem aeternam dona ei, Domine, et lux perpetua luceat ei. Requiescat in pace, Amen.*"

The priest concluded the funeral prayer with the sign of the cross and then rose and processed out. Henry waved the rest of the funeral party to follow the priest and to leave him there alone. When they had left him all alone in the candlelight, he got up and came closer to the tomb. The lid was a bronze effigy of Richard as he had been in life, and from Henry's memories, it captured his likeness fairly well. He had narrow delicate features, curly hair, and his beard was always sparse, his eyes sparkling as though he was always looking at a horde of jewels. He still had a crown on his head in the effigy, even though he had not died a king. That crown was now on Henry's head, the troublesome thing…

"…within the hollow crown
That rounds the mortal temples of a king
Keeps death his court…"

Richard had said this upon learning of his father's successful coup against him. Henry, as his young hostage, had watched the king giving into despair. They traveled eastward through north Wales and only got a little way before they met Bolingbroke the Usurper and his army and had to hold up in an old Norman fort. He remembered seeing sad Richard looking wistfully at the crown he had thrown off in shame. His bronze effigy carried the same wistful look, as if the whole defining moment of his life, his defeat, was forever immortalized on his tomb. Hal couldn't have done anything as a child to prevent it.

"More will I do:
Though all I can do is nothing worth;
Since that my penitence comes after all,
Imploring pardon." said Henry.

He heard faint footsteps approach him in the echoing vault. Only then did he notice how wet his eyes were.

"So, Richard is buried again," said his visitor.

Henry turned; the visitor was none other than Coris, the Storyteller: the narrator of tales and speaker of prologues with the golden voice that had the power to catch people up in his words and transport them to faraway realms.

"Where I soon shall follow," said Henry.

Henry looked over at the empty slabs and alcoves in the vault. Coris came closer and saw his tear-stained face in the candlelight. His heavy eyes were moved with pity. He made the sign of the cross and knelt on the other side of the tomb with the king.

"Richard's death was not your fault." said the Storyteller.

"Yet I have all the glory of his

Henry looked over at the empty slabs and alcoves in the vault. Coris came closer and saw his tear-stained face in the candlelight. His heavy eyes were moved with pity.

overthrow. It is the original sin of my father visited upon me... and it will be revenged upon my people." said Henry.

"You would not be king, Henry, if it were not God's will."

Henry smirked. God's will? Had it been His will before the Bard wrote about it? Was it the Bard's will or His? It must have been since He created the Bard. The way they spoke of the Bard made him seem like the all-powerful one, but it was a comforting thought that it was not the case. He looked back sadly at the effigy of Richard's face.

"It is time, my king." said the Storyteller.

Henry stood up in surprise.

"So soon?"

The Storyteller nodded. Henry posed himself, his heart racing, over the tomb of Richard II.

"Then begin it; the tomb of a king is a fitting place to begin where it shall end as well." said Henry.

The Storyteller came up to the candles lit beside the coffin and spread his arms wide like a conjurer.

"O for a muse of fire, that would ascend
The brightest heaven of invention..."

KING CHARLES INVITED THE WRONG PEOPLE

Lawrence "Mack" Hall

"He dispatched his servants to summon the invited guests to the feast, but they refused to come."
— Saint Matthew 22:3

In the British monarchy (1,500 years and still in business) the successor becomes monarch by the Grace of God, not by the gracelessness of a caucus or a TV network poll, immediately upon the death of his or her predecessor. The coronation changes nothing, but is instead a religious occasion reminding the king or queen that he or she is nothing without God. There are crowns and robes and processions and blessings, but "uneasy lies the head that wears the crown" (King Henry IV, Part II) because the theme inherent in the coronation liturgy is "Man, thou art dust, and to dust thou shalt return" (Genesis 3:19).

A king or a reigning queen is not an oligarch; the job comes with observable perks but also with twenty-four-hours of usually unseen obli-

gations to the people for the rest of the monarch's life. Some nice sets of wheels come with the gig but as we learn from history (you know, one of those irrelevant liberal arts), the king might ride in a nice carriage today but in a tumbril tomorrow.

A constitutional monarchy is not a Disney movie.

After the solemnities of the coronation itself, though, there are merriments and parties and parades and entertainments throughout the kingdom. King Charles invited a number of fashionable entertainers for some of the more fashionable parties, but most of them have refused the invitation. Somehow the cool kids J.K. Rowlinged them.

And that is probably a good thing. The city traders, three-passport-holders, cinema stars, three-chord commandos, transient oligarchs, and wealthy exiles from other nations have no loyalty to anything but their next business deal. And make no mistake, the musician in ragged jeans wailing comradely countercultural songs is Mr. Big Business indeed.

King Charles might learn from this embarrassment that the choristers of St. Michael's Church in Chesterton are loyal to the kingdom and to the person of the king; a famous chanteuse paid millions to entertain at an oil sheik's wedding might be less interested.

The United Kingdom and the Commonwealth nations are rich with church choirs, Girl Guides, Boy Scouts, amateur theatrical troupes, veterans' clubs, dance classes, marching bands, soloists, military bands, sea chanties from Newfoundland, the music and arts of Australia, the Bahamas, Belize, Canada, Grenada, Jamaica, New Zealand, Papua New Guinea, St. Kitts and Nevis, St. Lucia, St. Vincent and the Grenadines, the Solomon Islands, Tuvalu, Antigua and Barbuda, Scots pipers, Irish dancers, Welsh singers, and whatever it is that Cornishmen do.

These are people from all over the world who get their hands dirty working proper jobs and on weekends practice and celebrate their arts because they love what they do. They would be honored to share their gifts with their king.

The invitations to entertain at the coronations should have gone first to those who from overseas will host fundraisers for plane tickets for the local band, and those closer who will have to take a bus or a train to get to London, wrestling a tuba aboard while the driver fusses: "Get a move on, Alf; we ain't got all day!"

Invitations to the nabobs and poncies, brittle and self-indulgent in their ingratitude, perhaps should never have gone out at all.

"God save the king" is a noble sentiment, but a nobler one would be for the king to say, from his heart, "God save the British people."

A BASKET OF BREAD AND ROSES

Amanda Pizzolatto

Elizabeth filled her basket with whatever bread she could find. She just hoped she wouldn't be seen by members of the court. While her husband shared her desire and passion for helping the poor, she knew his family complained constantly about her works of mercy. They were already spreading rumors that she was stealing from them to take care of the poor. Though Elizabeth did have to admit to herself, she did think her in-laws had one necklace too many, among other things. But that thought would be put aside for another time, right now, she had to get this food to the poor and to get back to the castle before her husband and his hunting party returned. They were having a party that night. She placed some cloth over the basket and left the castle.

She walked towards the town, taking a shortcut through the woods. She didn't hear or see any horses. So far so good. However, she had only walked a few more feet before the sounds of the party reached her ears.

The hunting party showed up mere minutes later, bringing itself to a full stop inches from where she stood.

Ludwig, her husband, was at the front of the party, and recognized her instantly. "Why, Elizabeth, what are you doing out here?"

His brother, Heinrich, scoffed. "Stealing from you, brother, and giving your treasures to the filthy poor, that's what."

Ludwig shot his brother a cold stare. "The poor could do with a few treasures, brother, we have more than enough."

"Then what is in that basket?" asked one of Ludwig's fellow hunters.

"She wouldn't cover it if she wasn't stealing from you," sneered another.

Ludwig got down from his horse and walked to his wife. "My dear, may I show these men the contents of your basket to, ah, allay their fears?"

Elizabeth merely nodded. "Yes, my love."

Ludwig leaned in and kissed her cheek. He reached down and flung off the blanket, revealing dozens

Artwork: *St Elizabeth Distributing Alms* by Daniel Gran, 1736–1737

of lush roses. His party murmured, mostly with relief. One berated Heinrich.

"She was stealing from Ludwig, eh? At this rate, one shouldn't wonder if you were a real thief, as quickly as you accuse her."

Heinrich let out a growl and turned an icy stare at Elizabeth, but otherwise kept his tongue. Elizabeth only returned the look with a warm smile. Heinrich might be stingy and perhaps a little too overprotective of his family's wealth, but he was no thief, no more than she was.

Ludwig covered the basket again. "Shall I escort you to your destination, my dear?"

She shook her head, smiling with admiration in her eyes. "I will be fine. I will not be long. We still have our party tonight."

"That we do." He kissed her, but before he pulled back, she heard him whisper, "Lord, protect my wife." He squeezed her hand, then got back on his horse. "I shall see you upon your return. Come gentlemen. Hiya!"

The men rode on towards the castle and Elizabeth continued towards the village. She came across the first beggar right at the edge of the village and quickly pulled the blanket off. She smiled, the roses were once again bread. She pulled out a loaf and handed it to the beggar.

"Thank you, my princess."

She smiled. "My pleasure." She patted his shoulder before going further into the town. She distributed the bread quickly. Soon she was on her way back to the castle. But it was one of several clues to the fact that she was a saint.

Another legend states that one time, Elizabeth brought a leper into her room and laid him on the bed she and Ludwig shared. Ludwig's mother found out about it and was furious. She sought out her son and told him about the leper. The two went to his room. Ludwig opened the canopy, but did not see the leper. There, on his bed, was the crucified Christ. The vision vanished after a moment, leaving both Ludwig stunned.

Elizabeth continued with her charity towards the poor, her husband continuing to support her until he died. The two had been married for only six years and had three lovely children. But the children were to stay with their father's family while Elizabeth spent the last four years of her life as a kind of nun, more a tertiary, for while she took vows like a nun, she did not live in a convent like one. It was a long held belief that her confessor was far too harsh on her, but she followed his directions without question. That, along with her generosity, her love of God and the poor, her kindness, and those miracles led the Pope down the path of canonization. In May 1235, Pope Gregory IX formally canonized her as a saint, and people have been asking for her prayers ever since.

Oh blessed Elizabeth, shining example of generosity and kindness, speak to the Lord on our behalf. May we listen to His will and one day, join you both in Heaven.

The Sleep of King Arthur in Avalon
by Edward Burne-Jones, 1881-1898

TO HOLD THE MOUNTAINS IN MY HAND: A TALE OF BONNIE PRINCE CHARLIE

Ray E. Lipinski

The sound of cavalry charging, musket fire and exploding cannon thunder once again rocked the prince from his sleep. His forehead was covered in sweat and his sheets damp with perspiration. It was the third time this week he had experienced the same deafening dream with its haunting visions, and he could not get them out of his head. The prince waited a few moments, clutching a homespun blanket, with the images of a unicorn and a lion stitched on it— ironically, the symbol of Scotland and England. He waited another few minutes for his heartbeat to slow before getting out of bed and going to the wash basin to calm himself. He poured the cold water into the bowl and splashed it over his stubbly face. Looking in the mirror he grimaced at his reflection with a look of utter defeat. The rain had stilled to a quiet trickle and with the household still asleep, he decided to go outside. Looking out over the glen, the once distinguished and glorified

Charles Edward Stewart, nicknamed the Bonnie Prince, wept.

"How can I be delivered from this folly? How can I ever take my throne?"

"Your highness, you will catch your death if you remain outside, for there is a chill in the air," a voice from behind exclaimed.

Charles turned around and gave a half smile to the image of what had become his savior and champion over the last few days, Flora Macdonald. Standing like a Greek goddess in a pale-yellow chemise, barefoot, her dark hair slightly blowing in the wind, he had been swept away by her beauty from the moment they met. The prince had been on the run after the defeat of Culloden hiding in barns and pantries and hidden locations offered from those that still believed in his cause and right to the British throne. Flora had been one of those loyal followers and came to his rescue when he was an hour away from capture on the Isle of Lewis. With government

Artwork: *Prince Charles Edward Stuart, 1720 - 1788. Eldest Son of Prince James Francis Edward Stuart* by Allan Ramsay, ca. 1745

forces closing in, Flora helped him escape by disguising himself as her maid, "Betty Burke," and they sailed across the sea to Skye where they were currently staying.

"I find this my favorite time of day, the morning, the sunrise in all of its glory as if God is granting the world another chance from the mistakes of yesterday, a chance to do good again."

"Yes, a new day with new promises, my lord," said Flora.

Charles sighed. Even though there were still brave men that would never let the dream for an independent Scotland wither away and would fly his standard from any rampart, the horrors of Culloden and its aftermath infested his mind. Try as he might, he could not shake the grief that weighed on his soul. Retaliation from the British government had been swift and merciless, its force almost like a biblical plague. The Jacobites that had not been captured were quickly hunted down and shown no mercy. Patrols were a menace and now a familiar scene as they were stationed in villages and seen traveling constantly on the roadsides. Search and seizure without provocation was rampant, and anyone suspected of treason, even women and children, were imprisoned. Speaking Gaelic was forbidden, Highland dress was outlawed, and talk of clearances was sweeping across the land. The Highlands had been raped and scourged by its British parents, and their punishment was far from over.

Flora had gone inside and re-emerged with a woolen blanket that she wrapped around the prince. "Come back inside, my lord. I believe today we should hear from Captain O'Neil about your departure."

"I wish to go to the village today, for at the inn, there will be music, drink and conversation."

Flora scoffed. "Are you daft, my lord? Such drink will do you in and such conversation will lead you to the British gallows."

The prince raised his chin in defiance. "I am their prince, their rightful sovereign, their royal—"

"You are not prince to everyone. To some, you are a charlatan that has brought about wrought and ruin. Not to mention the bounty of 500 gold liveries for your capture that would tempt the most loyal of your subjects that are now mostly destitute," Flora reprimanded.

The prince held Flora's gaze. "You wound me, madame."

He turned around and gazed out over the rising sun. The purple thistles that were spread across the field now seemed to glow as the rays of the sun revealed their beauty, and they danced in the wind singing of a new day. Turning back around, he protested, "I once… I once held the mountains in my hand, from Ben Nevis to Glencoe with the victories of Prestonpans and Falkirk. We marched gloriously to Edinburgh, where the throne was in my grasp."

Flora softly replied, "Yes, my prince, and all is not lost in the dream of a free Scotland, but not in the rabble of a tavern."

"My beautiful Flora, how you make me want to go on."

With that notion, they agreed not to go into the village and Flora took his mind off things with a stroll by the lakeside. In the distance Charles could see the Scorrybreac mountains, their majesty towering gracefully above like angels' wings frozen in time.

He stared longingly and again repeated, "I once held the mountains in my hands, my army was great, my men noble, and Scotland was mine."

"My lord you are still a mighty prince whose quest is not lost. There is still talk of hidden Jacobite gold on the Isle of Chaney, and there are many noblemen in France and Italy that would see you on the throne. This is just a minor setback. Come inside and

I shall make some of those honey and oat cakes you have come to enjoy."

"My stomach leaps in anticipation, sweet Flora," replied the prince.

After their sumptuous feast, the rest of the prince's day was spent in his room, reading Chaucer, and going over the conversations he would have with his cousin James, the Duke of Liria, to regain support in Spain and the eastern provinces. He would also have to speak to the Paris bankers, John and George Waters, friends he had acquired before he landed in Scotland that had helped with financing the rebellion. Would they still assist him? Did they still have the confidence in him they once showed at the dinners and parties he hosted along his hilltop chateau in Montmarte in what seemed so long ago?

A knock on the door broke his contemplative thoughts and Flora appeared. "Your Highness, I bring news from Captain O'Neil. The fog coming from the western sea has settled over the bay, so he cannot attempt passage until the mid-morning, but a safe transport awaits you on the island of Raasay."

"And you will accompany me?" asked the prince.

"If it pleases Your Highness," Flora responded with a slight courtesy.

"Yes, you bring great comfort to me," said the prince with a smile.

By the evening, after another familiar rain, the prince's restlessness got the better of him, and he dressed to go to The Dog and Lady, the tavern and inn that had peaked his attention so many days ago. Flora argued with him for well more than an hour, citing what would happen to himself, her, and in

fact the entire village of Portree if he was captured. He dismissed her warnings and, borrowing a set of clothes from the owner of the house they were staying at, announced he was ready to attend the activities of the tavern. The prince stood there, quite proud of himself in his tan colored breeches, pale green shirt, and a stained white cravat that was not tied the right way.

Walking over to fix it, Flora scoffed. "You look ridiculous, my lord. You will not pass as a poor tenant farmer. Your cheeks are too delicate, and you look like you are about to address Parliament. I fear this night will end with us as fodder for the Kelpies."

> **Flora argued with him for well more than an hour, citing what would happen to himself, her, and in fact the entire village of Portree if he was captured.**

Flora was of course referencing the old Scottish folklore of the aquatic half-horse/half human spirits and their attraction to those in distress. The stories always ended deadly with some helpless hero or heroine being dragged to the depths of the sea at the hands of the tempestuous, disdainful creatures.

It was a short walk to The Dog and Lady, and other than running into the parson locking up for the night at St. Mila's, the village was as silent as the grave. Down a short cobblestone pathway and around a wooded corner lay the tavern, its two chimneys smoking away and bright lights welcoming any wayward stranger seeking shelter for the night. Flora and the prince ducked in quietly and immediately found a table far off in the corner. It was a typical two-story tavern with a staircase off to the side guiding patrons to their lodgings, and one immense open room with a large hearth in the middle with a double fireplace. Animal heads lined the walls along with family coats-of-arm plaques on the back wall along with a rather large skin of what looked like a Highland coo with a map of Skye etched on it. There were large wooden wagon wheels hanging from iron chains with pillared candles burning bright and a huge Scottish flag, the cross of St. Andrew tattered and worn inside a wooden frame with about twenty names, all men listed on it, with the Gaelic words "*I Gcuimhne*" ... In remembrance, being guarded vigilantly by two wooden stags on either side of the main wall.

The couple ordered drinks and cottage pie and settled down in each other's company, the prince telling Flora of his exploits at the siege of Gaeta in central Italy and coming under fire at the wee age of fourteen. A familiar voice startled Flora and she turned around in apprehension. Just as she had dreaded, on the other side of the hearth was Lacroix Duncan and his older brother Thaddeus. Flora and Thaddeus had briefly courted many years before and realized a friendship was far more preferable to marriage. Lacroix was the town mischief-maker and also sweet on Flora and she hoped he would not see her tonight and keep his distance. The prince was already on his second brandy and seemed to be enjoying taking in all the sights and sounds of the general merrymaking.

"Do you think a card game could be had with one of these gentlemen, sweet Flora?" asked Charles innocently.

"My lord, this is one step away from a village hovel, not a Parisian social club entertaining the Duke of Savoy. And besides...."

Their conversation was cut short when they heard the sound of breaking glass. The couple looked around just as Lacroix Duncan swiped two pints across the table, lunging at a lad sitting directly in front of him, broken glass and beer flying everywhere.

"I don't care about the cause. I hope they capture that bastard prince and burn him in a barn like a dirty rat."

The lad leaped across the table and was about to throw a blow at Lacroix until Thaddeus intervened, placing himself in between the two men.

"David, let it go. My brother is a drunken fool, but he is still my brother," exclaimed Thaddeus, giving David a deadening stare.

David took a few steps back. "Aye, it was those bloody redcoats that did this to us, blame them."

Lacroix screamed, pushed Thaddeus away and grabbed David by the shirt slamming him up against the wall.

"We were all there David, do you remember? Do you remember? General Murray told that halfwit prince to wait, to wait! Even if we had gone around through Culloden woods, we could have stood a chance, but no, that drunk Stewart waded us across that stinking field to our deaths. The wee bastard put us on a silver platter and delivered us right over to Cumberland to devour."

Tears swelled in Lacroix's eyes. David and Lacroix held each other's gaze for a moment. The room was silent. David placed his hand on Lacroix's shoulder and gave him a nod and both men embraced. Time stopped for a moment as two soldiers acknowledged a bond they would never forget. David exited the doorway, and the tavern came alive again with music and laughter.

"Come on brother, let's go home." replied Thaddeus as he led Lacroix towards the door. He caught a glimpse of Flora and then looked at the prince. For a moment it looked like Thaddeus was going to walk over to Flora but thought better of it. He gave Flora a hard stare and shook his head with disdain before going after his brother.

"We should make haste to the house, my lord. We have had quite the excitement for the evening." The prince agreed, and the "strange" couple left out a back door.

They walked in silence until they again came upon St. Mila's and the prince spoke. "It quite distresses me that my fellow subjects and compatriots think of me with such contempt."

Flora stopped dead in her tracks. With her back facing the prince, she exhaled sharply and turned around. "Lacroix's men were with Cameron's regiment. They were the first to lead the charge. Lacroix, Thaddeus, and Dennis, their wee brother of eighteen. Dennis died of cannon fire with his intestines falling out with one arm already having been blown off. When his wife, who was pregnant, came to collect his body the day after, she was run through by a British patrol. So yes, with all due respect, Charles, if I was one of them, I'd want to see you in a burning barn as well. Men talk of war with such gallantry, making it sound so grand and noble, but it is just a senseless game that little boys play where no one wins. Yes, my lord, I will be in rebellion against English tyranny until the day I die, but oh, if you had just waited and listened to Lord Murray, I believe we would not be in this predicament."

Flora turned back around and gasped as David was standing right in front of her.

"Flora Macdonald, what.... why…?" David looked past her at the prince. Flora stammered for something to say but could not think of any words. David walked closer to the prince. "I fought with Clan Cameron that day, Your Highness. I was on your left flank." David stepped back and gave a slight bow and then disappeared across the church yard.

"Thank you, soldier," the prince whispered. The couple continued their journey back to the farmhouse without another word between them.

It was just before midnight when the prince heard a slight knocking at his door. He opened it, and there was Flora, in a cream-colored chemise this time, hair falling by her shoulders, carrying a single candle holder and a wee knapsack asking to come in.

"Are you ready for your final leg of the journey, my lord?"

"Yes, in three days' time, I will be looking down from the Grampian Mountains and expect to be walking the halls of Versailles by September."

"A worthy goal, my lord," Flora replied as she placed the candle on the nearby table. "I have made some honey and oat cakes for your journey and this, for you to remember me by…"

Flora handed him a white handkerchief with blue thistles embroidered around the edges.

"'Tis beautiful like you, Flora. I will cherish it always as I will cherish you and the memory of these last few days. But I need no reminder of you. I will keep these days in my heart forever."

The prince took her hand and pulled her into a close embrace, kissing her softly. He paused, not wanting to offend her, but she guided him closer to the bed and blew out the candle.

Flora had left the prince's room shortly before daybreak not wanting to confuse or complicate any more emotions that had flooded both her and the prince over the last couple of days. He walked out of the house under his guise of Betty Burke and walked over to the chicken coup where Flora was waiting. She held her stomach as she looked away trying not to laugh.

"I am so glad I can offer you a source of amusement, my kind lady," mused the prince.

"Oh, my Lord, I told you that your… disguise would not fool anyone. You still look quite ridiculous."

"Nonsense! Little Katie added just enough rouge on my cheeks, and this straw wig makes me a beautiful dame indeed!" chuckled Charles.

"Hmmm, whatever you say… my queen," responded Flora.

It was a short ride to the dock at Portree and Captain O'Neil was already waiting with the skiff that would take him to the ship bound for Raasay. With a good wind and strong tide, they would reach their destination by nightfall. At the dock, the prince removed his hood and kissed Flora on the cheek.

"Perhaps you will be my queen longer than a night when I return to take up the cause again," suggested the prince.

Flora smiled. "Just remember, my lord, you once held the mountains in your hand."

She stepped away, gave a deep curtsey, and then watched as the boat with the 'Young Pretender' disappeared over the sea from Skye.

The prince would have a few more adventures before he finally escaped from Scotland. British spies along with a certain anonymous tip about a tavern brawl would keep him on the run for a few more weeks. Playing hide-and-go-seek among the isles and mountain encampments kept him in flight, avoiding near capture in the glens. Then, on September 29, he found himself on the French frigate *L'Heureux* where he said a final goodbye to a Scotland he would never return to. Looking out over the deck, he pulled his waistcoat closer to him as a cold breeze blew in from the south. The ship's sails were full, and as the vessel sailed past the shores of Loch nan Uamh, the Bonnie Prince Charles Edward Stuart hummed a song from his childhood of a noble warrior in a far-off land that slayed a dragon, rescued a maiden, found a treasure, and was crowned king by a grateful nation.

He smiled and said to himself as the last view of Scotland dipped beneath the horizon, "I once held the mountains in my hand."

The Skye Boat Song
Robert Louis Stevenson (1892)

Sing me a song of a lad that is gone,
Say, could that lad be I?
Merry of soul he sailed on a day
Over the sea to Skye.
Mull was astern, Rùm on the port,
Eigg on the starboard bow;
Glory of youth glowed in his soul;
Where is that glory now?
Give me again all that was there,
Give me the sun that shone!
Give me the eyes, give me the soul,
Give me the lad that's gone!
Billow and breeze, islands and seas,
Mountains of rain and sun,
All that was good, all that was fair,
All that was me is gone.
Sing me a song of a lad that is gone,
Say, could that lad be I?
Merry of soul he sailed on a day
Over the sea to Skye.

Portrait of Louis XIV
by Hyacinthe Rigaud, ca. 1700

CORONATION EMBLEM: SYMBOL OF CHALLENGES AND OPPORTUNITIES FOR A NEW ERA

Wesley Hutchins

The passing of Her Late Majesty Queen Elizabeth II on September 8, 2022, marked the end of an era—the Second Elizabethan Era, personified by her grace, dignity, and commitment to duty and service, especially with being from the Greatest Generation that served in World War II.

In a letter I sent to the Queen on September 3, I conveyed my congratulations on her Platinum Jubilee, as well as my admiration and respect for her decades of service to the United Kingdom, the Commonwealth, and beyond. Furthermore, I also wrote:

"While Your Majesty may not be seen as much in public as in the past, that is quite understandable, and indeed, Your Majesty does deserve to relax and be at ease after more than 70 years of being steadfast to the promise Your Majesty made at age 21 to devote Your Majesty's life, 'whether it be long or short,' to the service of Your Majesty's people, and therein lies something to which all of us should look to as a model for our own lives.

Even in the depths of a once-in-a-century pandemic, Your Majesty's dedication was quite admirable, and if I may say so, your speech in the early days of the pandemic, with its reference to Vera Lynn's 'We'll Meet Again,' was comforting and resonating at that particularly bleak time. Your continued dedication to service via virtual means is a remarkable testament to the technological advances that have taken place over the course of Your Majesty's remarkable reign and lifetime."

With much regret, that letter did not arrive in time before the Queen's passing. Now, with the accession of King Charles III—whose apprenticeship as his mother's heir-apparent and Prince of Wales was the longest in British history—we are now in a new Carolean Age. With that has come changes

Artwork: *Arms, flag, and standard of the United Kingdom of Great Britain and Ireland* by Royal College of Arms, 1800

in iconography, currency, post/pillar boxes, and gender designations from female to male. These changes will take time getting used to, thanks to the Queen's 70-year reign, which made her the only British monarch most of us had ever known.

Among the new icons unveiled in this new Carolean Era is the emblem for the King's Coronation at Westminster Abbey on May 6, 2023. It unifies the floral emblems of the four home nations of the United Kingdom; the rose of England, the thistle of Scotland, the daffodil of Wales, and the shamrock of Northern Ireland. They pay tribute to the King's love of the natural world and together, they create the shape of St. Edward's Crown, with which Charles III will be crowned during the coronation service.

As a person for whom the unity of the United Kingdom has been important, this emblem for the coronation is particularly meaningful. It is a demonstration to the world and perhaps even to people in the UK itself that the UK is not, and has never been, just England, and that the UK has always been the sum of its constituent parts through a complex web of history, individual contributions, collective sacrifice, and shared experiences that are as interwoven as the coronation emblem itself. Indeed, there is something quite special about this diversity, which has become richer through immigration from the Commonwealth and other places, and the King himself has spoken repeatedly about Britain's many communities and their respective importance to British national life.

The monarchy itself has been at the heart of national life for over a thousand years. It is therefore an ancient institution that represents the good, the bad, the ugly, the truth of what Britain is, and can be, as a nation. It is the connection between Britain's past and present, and therefore has an obligation to constructively bring all Britons together in a shared future that is sure to be more complex. Whilst representing tradition, it also weaves a delicate balance with modernity as British society evolves and changes. This penchant for flexibility and adaptation has been a hallmark of the monarchy, and the King is expected to continue in this tradition.

In this light, the coronation emblem—designed using the red, white, and blue of the Union Flag—is rooted in ancient iconography for a new era in which the religious, social, cultural, and ethnic diversity of the United Kingdom may be effectively acknowledged and celebrated within the context of great British traditions, such as the coronation itself. Indeed, the coronation service, whilst still an Anglican service at its heart, is supposed to reflect the nature of the UK in 2023 with the incorporation of diverse elements of modern British society. This is consistent with the King in his role as Supreme Governor of the Church of England and Defender of the Faith, but also showing respect toward other faiths. Additionally, there are other events meant to bring people and communities together throughout the country for this historic occasion in a display of unity which the monarchy is supposed to inculcate.

Over the course of her 70-year reign, the Queen strived to represent such unity and she gained the admiration and respect of many people, including those who are indifferent or otherwise against the monarchy as an institution. The great test going forward will be to transfer that admiration and respect to her heirs and successors, so that a vast cross-section of the UK will continue to see the monarchy as worth maintaining, as well as relevant to their present and future.

This may prove deeply challenging due to the current state of affairs in the UK, namely the fractures and controversies within the Royal Family and throughout British society more broadly, with the social, political, and economic dislocations of recent years that have brought fresh scrutiny unto many aspects of British life, including the monarchy itself, particularly among younger Britons. The colonial legacy, out of which were born the Empire and Commonwealth, is another issue which must be robustly addressed going forward by the monarchy, given its role—direct and indirect—in said legacy. Furthermore, whereas the Queen came to the throne at 25 years old and remained much of an enigma to the end, her son is 74 and a lot is known about him, with perceptions of him being firmly established among most of the public for better or worse.

This is not to say that it's all doom and gloom for the monarchy, if for no other reason than the institution has been here before, with questions about its fitness and future amid societal, political, and economic shifts. However, the increasingly multi-ethnic, multi-faith, and secular composition of the UK makes the situation more complicated, and the monarchy will have to balance the needs of multiple constituencies that are as intertwined as the components of the coronation emblem to create something that is the total sum of the United Kingdom.

Therefore, this ancient institution and the embodiment of Britishness is facing a major test of its penchant for flexibility and adaptability in the twenty-first century without the much-beloved Elizabeth II at the helm. One can only hope with utmost sincerity that Charles III—trained to the hilt over seven decades and with well-established capabilities—will rise to the occasion and that the unity expressed symbolically in this coronation emblem will become realized in due time, during the coronation weekend and beyond. In summation, it does represent the complexities of the past and the hope for the future.

KINGSHIP IN THE OLD TESTAMENT, NEW TESTAMENT AND WHAT IT MEANS FOR KINGS TODAY

Llewelyn Lawton

Old Testament

Kingship in the Pentateuch

The first time that kings are mentioned in Scripture is in Genesis 14. In this text, the kings of Shinar, Ellasar, Elam, and Hoiim are at war with the kings of Sodom, Gomorrah, Admah, and Zeboiim, and the Patriarch Abraham (Abram) and his nephew Lot were caught in the middle of the conflict. This war has the usual pitfalls of Ancient Near Eastern warfare: goods and people are seized, and even those who are unaligned innocent parties (Lot) are captured. Using the hermeneutic paradigm of reading scriptural narrative as moral law at this point (Genesis 14:1-16), it would not be a leap to take this as a rejection of kings: Violence of this level has not been seen since the flood, and why has it happened here? It is because of greedy warmongering kings. Next, however, the narrator introduces Abraham and us to another king, Melchizedek, King of Salem (Genesis 14:17-20). Melchizedek means either "King of Righteousness" or "My King is Righteousness," and Salem is a short form of Jerusalem and means Peace. Melchizedek is nothing like the other kings; he is righteous, and unlike the warring kings we had just met, the name of his kingdom is Peace. On top of this, he is a Priest of Abraham's God, and gives Abraham a meal of Bread and Wine, blesses him, and receives a tithe from him. In Melchizedek, we see a different model of kingship, which is priestly and about serving, not ruling. Later, in Genesis 17, God promises Abraham and Sarah that among their offspring will be kings of nations. Two generations passed, and the Hebrews did not yet have a king; one of their number was, however, a servant to the king in Egypt (Genesis 41:37-45). Four generations later, the king of the Egyptians began to oppress the Israelites, so Moses led them out.

When Moses led Israel out of Egypt, the governance structure was

Artwork: *David and Abigail* by Avanzino Nucci, 1620s

not monarchical but a set of judges adjudicating over the people in sections of thousands, hundreds, fifties, and tens. In Numbers 23:21, it is noticed by the Gentile prophet Balam that the reason the Israelites are victorious and without trouble is because "The LORD their God is with them, acclaimed as a king among them." For the Israelites, after the Exodus, they did not need a king as they had the LORD as king. However, It is worth noting that Moses' law does have a provision for Israel to appoint a king over them (Deuteronomy 17:14-20). The provision makes the following commandments for the king and their appointment:

- The King will be chosen by the LORD (15a).
- He must be an Israelite, not a foreigner (15b).
- He must not acquire horses, especially not from Egypt (16).
- He must not acquire many wives, that is he is to be monogamous (17a)
- He must not acquire silver and gold (17b)
- He must have a copy of the Law to study all the days of his life (18-19)
- He must not exalt himself over other Israelites (20a)
- He must closely adhere to the LORD's Commandments (20b)

The king described by these rules is the polar opposite of Ancient Near Eastern kings who were often foreign, with large cavalries, hoarding wives and riches, and exalting themselves above their subjects and the laws of their land. This provision was not a command to make a king. Instead, it was a concession for when Israel, out of hard-heartedness, decides to appoint a king like those around them. So, from the time of Jacob through to the time of Samson, the last of the Judges, Israel had no human king to rule over them as they were meant to rely on the LORD as their king.

Kings in Israel

The appointment of King Saul came not from a command from the LORD. Instead, it was a demand from the people. The Israelites felt weak compared to their neighbours and thought they were not being appropriately governed. They wanted a king to lead and protect them (1 Samuel 8:5). Samuel warned them this would be a rejection of the kingship of the LORD and that the king they would appoint would exploit the people rather than protect them (1 Samuel 8:10-18). Nevertheless, Israel demanded a king and sent Samuel to find one for them (1 Samuel 8:19-22). So they picked Saul, the son of a wealthy man. Saul was handsome and a whole head taller than any other man in the community of Israel (1 Samuel 9). Saul was a man that seemed to fit with the people's image of a king, the type their Gentile neighbours have.

But Saul wasn't a good king. Instead, he disobeyed the commands of the LORD (1 Samuel 15:11). For a series of stories of how Saul consistently failed to live up to God's standards for a king, read 1 Samuel 13-15. At the core of Saul's disobedience is self-exaltation, which could be seen as a summation of the eight rules of Deuteronomy 17. Israelite kings are meant to be the opposite of the Gentile kings, but Saul acted precisely like them.

So God sent Samuel to find a king after God's own heart—a king who relied on God for his strength, not armies and horses, who would exalt the LORD and protect his people. Unlike when Samuel anointed Saul, Samuel found the right man for the job in David, the youngest son of Jesse of Bethlehem (1 Samuel 16:1-13). David was not a great warrior: he was a shepherd who spent his spare time playing the lyre and writing poetry.

David grew up to be a great king over Israel. However, he did have his failings: he murdered his soldier

Uriah to cover up the adultery with Bathsheba (2 Samuel 11-12), he committed polygamy (2 Samuel 3:2-5, 1 Chronicles 3:1-9), took a census of his men (2 Samuel 24:1-17), and he did not correctly discipline or govern his sons leading to rebellion (1 Kings 1:6, 2:13-25). However, unlike Saul before him, he repented; Psalm 51 is a prayer of repentance after his affair with Bathsheba, 2 Samuel 12:13 tells of Nathan's rebuke of David and his subsequent repentance, and 1 Chronicles 21:8-17 tells of David's repentance over the census taking. God promised David that he would have a descendent who would rule on the Throne of Judah forever (2 Samuel 7:16)

After David's death, he is succeeded by his son Solomon (1 Kings 1-2). Solomon was known for his wisdom (1 Kings 3:5-14), his building projects, especially the Jerusalem temple (1 Kings 5-9), his riches, and his visit from the Queen of Sheba.

Solomon, like his father, did not follow the law relating to monogamy, leading to his apostasy and downfall in his old age (1 Kings 11:9-10).

In David and Solomon, we great men of faith who make great kings but end up going astray, relying on and pursuing earthly power, riches, and women rather than relying on and pursuing the LORD.

The rest of the story of Israel's kings is much the same as the above, great kings rise up, but at the end of the day, no human king is faithful to God's plan. The desire for a godly king and Messiah that is the anointed one who will save God's people and bring about God's kingdom was unmet.

> They do not find this king in Herod's palace; they find him in the small town of Bethlehem. The king they find is an infant, Jesus, Mary's son. They hail him as King.

New Testament

Birth and Genealogy

Fast forward to circa 1 AD, and we find the Roman client kingdom of Judea. Now the king of Judea at this time was Herod the Great; Herod was not a descendant of David; in fact, his parents were not even Judeans, his father was an Edomite, and his mother was a Nabatean.

On top of this, he relied on foreign soldiers, amassed wealth and wives for himself, was disobedient to the Laws of God, and treated his subjects with disdain. Herod was a king in complete disobedience to Deuteronomy's Law concerning kings.

Early in the Gospels, we are introduced to two subjects of King Herod, called Joseph and Mary. They were not government officials or in high standing in the realm, but they were both descendants of David (Matthew 1:1-17, Luke 3:23-38), devout servants of the LORD.

Mary is visited by the Angel of Gabriel, who tells her that she will give birth to a son who "will be great, and will be called the Son of the Most High, and the Lord God will give to him the throne of his ancestor David. He will reign over the house of Jacob forever, and of his kingdom there will be no end." (Luke 1:32-33). Mary's son will be a king like David, but unlike David, he will reign forever and be the Son of God.

In Matthew's Gospel (2:1-12), we hear of the Magi, wise men of the east, who see signs of a new great King of the Jews. They do not find this king in Herod's palace; they find him in the small town of Bethlehem. The king they find is an infant, Jesus, Mary's son. They hail him as King.

Ministry and Teaching

In his preaching and teaching, Jesus refers to himself as the "Son of Man" and is referred to as the Messiah/Christ by his followers; both of these terms are used in the Old Testament to refer to the promised Davidic king.

In his preaching, he preached about the kingdom of God or kingdom of Heaven and that it was close at hand (Matthew 4:17, Luke 10:9). He referred to his kingdom (i.e. Mark 6:23, Luke 22:30, John 18:36). His parables often referenced the kingdom (Matthew 13:31-31, 13:44, 13:45-46, and Luke 17:20-21).

In his ministry, he demonstrated his unique way of being king: Jesus humbled himself by washing his disciples' feet, a task typically reserved for servants. He then instructed his disciples to follow his example and serve one another (John 13:1-17). Jesus fed a crowd of over 5,000 people with just five loaves of bread and two fish. He did not send them away hungry but served them by providing food (Matthew 14:13-21). Throughout the Gospels, Jesus healed the sick and showed compassion to those suffering. Jesus instructed his disciples that the greatest among them would be the one who serves others, not the one who seeks power or authority (Matthew 20:20-28).

Holy Week

Holy Week is the week between Palm Sunday and Easter Sunday and takes up a large portion of the Gospels. In the Holy Week narratives, Jesus models and proclaims his kingship in the following five ways: Triumphal Entry: Jesus entered Jerusalem on a donkey, fulfilling the prophecy of Zechariah 9:9, "Behold, your king is coming to you, humble, and mounted on a donkey." An action that simultaneously demonstrated his kingship and humility; he was a king but not a mighty warrior riding in pomp and ceremony.

When Judas betrayed Jesus, he did not resist or retaliate. Instead, he calmly allowed the events to unfold, showing his willingness to be a sacrifice for the sake of others (Matthew 26:47-56). Throughout his trial and crucifixion, Jesus modelled servant leadership by offering forgiveness, compassion, and care for others. He prayed for his persecutors, saying, "Father, forgive them, for they know not what they do" (Luke 23:34). At his trial and crucifixion, Jesus was proclaimed and crowned king. Pilate is portrayed as calling Jesus a king (Matthew 27:11). While whipping and mocking Jesus the Roman soldiers hailed him as King of Jews, crowned him with a crown of thorns, and dressed him in a scarlet robe (Matthew 27:27-31). The charge they nailed above Jesus on the Cross proclaimed him as "Jesus of Nazareth, King of the Jews" in Hebrew, Greek, and Latin (John 19:19-20). Even those watching and mocking him referred to him as "King of Israel" (Matthew 27:42).

Jesus' crucifixion was a coronation. The son of man was lifted high, not in an earthly or pompous way; he did not exalt himself above others; instead, he was lifted up on the Cross and exalted by those who hated him.

Christian Kings

So how should a Christian king rule? A Christian king must remember these three following things: First, they are not the highest authority; above them is Jesus, the King of Kings, who they are called to be servants of. British monarchs and their Anglican subjects are reminded of this in the communion liturgy of the Book of Common Prayer:

"ALMIGHTY God, whose kingdom is ever-lasting, and power infinite: Have mercy upon the whole Church; and so rule the heart of thy chosen servant CHARLES, our King and Governor, that he (knowing whose minister he is) may above all things seek thy honour and glory: and that we and all his subjects (duly considering whose authority he hath) may faithfully serve, honour, and humbly obey him, in thee, and for thee, according to thy blessed Word and ordinance; through Jesus Christ our Lord, who with thee and the Holy Ghost liveth and reigneth, ever one God, world without end. Amen."

Secondly, in serving Christ, they must look to his way of leading and follow his example. That is not exalting themselves above others but being a servant of the people, putting others' needs before their own and pointing the nation to God.

Finally, they must pattern and shape their lives on the instructions of Scripture and obey God's command-ments. While not all of the Deuteron-omy passage is relevant to Christian Monarchs today (relying on Egyptian Horses wouldn't have the same impact in wars), they still act as an important guideline.

So how shall a Christian king act?

- He shall remember that he is subject to King Jesus.
- He shall follow Christ's model of servant kingship.
- He shall not rely on his armies for their strength.
- He shall not take on multiple wives or have mistresses.
- He shall not amass large amounts of personal wealth.
- He shall daily study Holy Scripture.
- He shall not exalt himself above his nation but serve and represent them.
- He shall act in accordance with God's moral law.

"NOW COME THE DAYS OF THE KING!": ARAGORN AS A FIGURE OF CHRIST THE KING

Thomas J. McIntyre

John Ronald Ruel (hereafter referred to as J.R.R.) Tolkien, author of the epic *Lord of the Rings* saga, was a devout Catholic. He passed to his eternal reward in 1973, almost four years after the implementation of Mass of Pope Paul VI, more commonly referred to as the *Novus Ordo Missae* (Latin: "New Order of the Mass"). Being the linguist that he was, Tolkien strongly preferred the Traditional Latin Mass, more commonly referred to as the Tridentine Rite. His grandson, Simon, reported that Tolkien continued to make the responses at Mass, loudly, in Latin, apparently oblivious to the rest of the congregation doing so in English.

With his apparently strong attraction to the Latin Mass, one might consider Tolkien to have been a "Traditionalist," a term often used to describe Catholics who are suspicious or even outright opposed to the changes that occurred in the Church, particularly in regards to liturgy, following the Second Vatican Council. However, most Traditionalists are monarchists, opposed to the new democratic forms of government that sprung up from the late eighteenth century until the twentieth. Tolkien was very much not a monarchist. In fact, he stated the following regarding not just monarchy but government in general: "The most improper job of any man, even saints (who at any rate were at least unwilling to take it on), is bossing other men. Not one in a million is fit for it, and least of all those who seek the opportunity."

One might see evidence of this negative view of monarchy in Tolkien's work. After all, the line of kings becomes corrupt and broken, with the failures of kings leading to catastrophe for Middle-Earth multiple times. Yet, the final redemption, and indeed salvation, of Middle-Earth is accomplished not by the rejection of monarchial government but in its restoration—the eponymous Return of the King in the person of Aragon, son of Arathorn, who rules the reunified kingdoms of

Artwork: *Christ Pantocrator mosaic from Hagia Sophia* by unknown artist, ca. 1261

Gondor and Arnor as High King Elessar. One might question how this major theme in Tolkien's epic connects with his stated belief in the impropriety of men "bossing other men." The key point is Tolkien's specification that such a job is improper to man. The implication of course is that it is improper to a *mere* man. If that man is a god, it might be a different story. Thus, the reader can understand that Aragorn is a Christ-figure, one of three in the *Lord of the Rings*.

Unlike the fantasy writings of his close friend and fellow Inkling, C.S. Lewis, Tolkien did not intend for his epic to be a direct allegory. Thus, one character can be a type of multiple Biblical figures. Frodo's steadfastly loyal companion Samwise Gamgee, for example, serves as an image both of St. John the Beloved Disciple and Simon of Cyrene. Conversely, one figure from salvation history can be represented by multiple characters. Different aspects of Our Lady are represented by Galadriel, Eowyn, and Arwen, while the threefold mission of Christ as Priest, Prophet, and King is represented by Frodo, Gandalf, and Aragorn respectively. Specifically, Aragorn is a type of Christ the King.

Christ the King

The Catholic Feast of Our Lord, Jesus Christ the King was established by Pope Pius XI in 1925 with his encyclical *Qua Primas*. At that time, communist and fascist ideologies were running rampant and regimes built on such ideologies were steadily gaining power even in Catholic countries like Spain, Mexico, and Italy. The pontiff explained his reasons for establishing the feast, writing:

When once men recognize, both in private and in public life, that Christ is King, society will at last receive the great blessings of real liberty, well-ordered discipline, peace and harmony... That these blessings may be abundant and lasting in Christian society, it is necessary that the kingship of our Savior should be as widely as possible recognized and understood, and to the end nothing would serve better than the institution of a special feast in honor of the Kingship of Christ. (19, 21)

The feast was originally celebrated on the last Sunday of October. This was meant to emphasize that Christ is Lord over both Heaven *and* Earth. Honoring Christ as King *before* the celebration of the Church Triumphant on All Saints' Day and beginning the period of praying for the souls of all the faithful departed, starting on All Souls' Day, in November, demonstrates that even before the end when Christ returns in glory, He reigns as King, not just over hearts and minds but over the nations of the earth.

The aforementioned liturgical reform that followed the Second Vatican Council moved the feast (now a Solemnity) of Christ the King to the last Sunday of the liturgical year, meaning it falls on one of the last two Sundays of November, with the next Sunday being the first of the season of Advent. In this way, the Second Coming of Christ is linked to His first. The liturgical readings from All Saints Day onward are eschatological in nature, focusing on being prepared for the return of Christ in glory and the judgment He will mete out. The readings of the first two Sundays of Advent continue this eschatological theme, although the Gospel reading for the Second Sunday begins the shift to preparation for our celebration of the first coming of Christ at Christmas.

Although the Solemnity of Christ the King is a movable feast (it occurs on a different date every year, unlike Christmas which is always on the same date), at the time when Tolkien was writing *The Fellowship of Ring*, it would have always fallen around the date of October 25. Therefore, it is quite interesting that it is at the Council that Strider's true identity as Aragorn, son of Arathorn, right king of Gondor is revealed. It is even more interesting that although it is decided at the Council that the Ring will be taken into Mordor to be cast into the fires of Mount Doom, the Fellowship waits two months before undertaking their quest.

The Fellowship departs from Rivendell on December 25 which is, of course, Christmas. Their mission is accomplished precisely three months later on March 25, which is the date of the Annunciation and therefore the Incarnation of Our Lord. However, March 25 was also the traditional date of Our Lord's Passion and Death (although Good Friday falls on a different date every year because Easter, like Christ the King, is a movable feast). Thus, the mission of the salvation of Middle Earth, carried out by three Christ-figures who each represent one of the threefold aspects of Our Lord's ministry as priest, prophet, and king, begins on Christmas and ends on the traditional date of Our Lord's Passion.

This makes the time spent in Rivendell preparing to embark on the journey to Mordor a sort of Advent. Most interestingly, Tolkien's linkage of the feast of Christ the King with the beginning of Advent by his dating of the Council of Elrond, shows that his thinking was more in line with the new liturgical calendar than the old, despite his documented preference for the Traditional Latin Mass.

The Paths of the Dead: Aragorn and the Harrowing of Hell

An interesting moment occurs towards the midpoint of *The Return of the King*. Having received Gondor's call for aid against the approaching armies of Sauron, the host of Rohirrim are riding to relieve the siege. With them is Aragorn, who is returning to claim his throne. On the eve of battle, however, Aragorn leaves the camp of Rohan in order to "walk the Paths of the Dead" and recruit an army of souls to fight against Sauron.

While at first glance, it might appear that Aragorn is engaging in some kind of necromancy by summoning an army of the dead to fight Sauron; this scene actually deepens the Catholic theme of Tolkien's masterpiece, rather than overturning it. Aragorn's eponymous return has obvious apocalyptic overtones, with the king who has been away from his throne so long, and appointed stewards to rule in his stead, finally returning to save his people from the overwhelming force of the Enemy that threatens to destroy them. However, especially paired with Frodo's journey into Mordor and the destruction of the Ring on March 25 (traditional date of Our Lord's Passion and Death), there are aspects to the first coming of Our Lord that are typified in Aragorn's arrival as well.

For example, in the book, Aragorn does not enter the city of Minas Tirith immediately after the Battle of the Pelennor Fields but instead sends heralds throughout the surrounding areas announcing his coming and gathering forces for the last stand at the Black Gate. There is a certain triumphal entry quality to this. Aragorn's journey on the Paths of the Dead and summoning the dead to fight for him against Sauron fits into this context as well.

The Apostles' Creed states that "He descended into Hell." The Catechism of the Catholic Church explains:

> Scripture calls the abode of the dead, to which the dead Christ went down, "hell" —*Sheol* in Hebrew or *Hades* in Greek—because those who are there are deprived of the vision of God. Such is the case for all the dead, whether evil or righteous, while they await the Redeemer: which does not mean that their lot is identical, as Jesus shows through the parable of the poor man Lazarus who was re-

ceived into "Abraham's bosom": "It is precisely these holy souls, who awaited their Savior in Abraham's bosom, whom Christ the Lord delivered when he descended into hell." Jesus did not descend into hell to deliver the damned, nor to destroy the hell of damnation, but to free the just who had gone before him (CCC 633)

In his first epistle, St. Peter writes that Our Lord, "went and preached to the spirits in prison" (3:19). Generally, at least biblically speaking, prisons are temporary and a person is released once they have paid the just sentence for their infractions. Another name for the place to which Our Lord descended is Limbo, which has come to mean a "state of waiting."

Despite this, medieval thought (by which Tolkien was heavily influenced) still saw Limbo or Sheol as part of the realm of Satan. Limbo is the first circle of Hell in Dante's famous *Inferno*. Medieval legends developed and apocryphal stories were written to expound on the brief description of this event in Scripture, which came to be called the Harrowing of Hell. The name of the location of Rohan's camp, from which Aragorn and his companions begin their journey on the Paths of the Dead, is Dunharrow.

In the book, Aragorn's waking of the dead to fight is part of the prophecy of the return of the heir of Isildur, the king who cut the Ring from the hand of Sauron in the Second Age. When Eowyn tries to dissuade Aragorn from taking the Paths of the Dead, Aragorn tells her "I go on a path appointed" (*Return of the King*, Chapter 2: "The Passing of the Grey Company," p. 46).

In the book, Aragorn also explains to Gimli the identity of the dead whom he will summon to fight against Sauron.

But the oath they broke was to fight against Sauron, and they must fight therefore, if they are to fulfill it. For at Erech there stands yet a black stone that was brought, it was said, from Númenor by Isildur, and it was set upon a hill, and upon it the King of the Mountains swore allegiance to him in the beginning of the realm of Gondor. But when Sauron returned and grew in might again, Isildur summoned the Men of the Mountains to fulfill their oath, and they would not: for they had worshipped Sauron in the Dark Years. (*Return of the King*, Chapter 2: "The Passing of the Grey Company," pg. 44)

Aragorn is not engaging in necromancy in order to raise an army of the dead to fight Sauron. As king of Gondor, he has the authority to lift the curse imposed by his ancestor Isildur. This would be similar to the difference between a priest asking questions of a demon in the course of an exorcism and a random civilian attempting to inquire of the same demon. Moreover, this lifting of the curse is actually part of his messianic mission of saving Gondor, as it has been prophesied.

Aragorn's power comes from being the prophesied "Heir of Isildur," a great though flawed king who is his ancestor. In the Gospels, Christ is referred to as the "Son of David," who was also a flawed though nevertheless great king, of whom Christ is a descendant. In Christian theology, all the human beings who had ever lived until the death of Our Lord had been held in the realm of the dead due to the curse imposed as a result of the sin of Adam and Eve, and were thus not at rest. The important difference, of course, is that Aragorn announces to the dead that they have a chance to redeem themselves and gain their rest, while Christ announces to the "spirits in the prison" that He had redeemed them and they could now be at rest. This fits with Tolkien's theme of not having perfect figures of Christ, in order to emphasize that these Christ figures are not actually Christ.

The Hands of the King Bring Healing

Being an Englishman, Tolkien would have been quite familiar with the legends surrounding St. Edward the Confessor, the last king of England before the Norman conquest (1042-1066). He is referred to as the Confessor to differentiate him from an earlier King Edward, called the Martyr, who was assassinated in 978. Even before his death, Edward was considered saintly, and it was said that he had the power to heal the disease scrofula, a form of tuberculosis called "the king's evil." This healing is immortalized by William Shakespeare (himself a Catholic, albeit a secret one) in his tragedy *Macbeth*. After the eponymous Scottish lord commits regicide by assassinating Duncan and usurps the throne, Malcom, the rightful heir, flees to the English court of King Edward. When the tyrant Macbeth murders MacDuff's wife and children, the latter joins his rightful king in exile. It is there that Duncan tells MacDuff of Edward's famed power to heal.

Tolkien incorporated this idea into his portrayal of Aragorn in *The Return of the King*. When Faramir and Éowyn are brought to the Houses of Healing in Minas Tirith after their respective encounters with the Nazgûl, the wizard Gandalf overhears the words of Ioreth, an elderly woman:

> "Would that there were kings in Gondor, as there were once upon a time, they say! For it is said in old lore: hands of the king are the hands of the healer. And so the rightful king could ever be known." (*Return of the King*, Chapter 7: "The Houses of Healing," pg. 138)

After coming to Gondor's aid and bringing victory in the Battle of the Pelennor Fields, Aragorn is hiding his true identity as the rightful king of Gondor and has his troops camp outside of Minas Tirith. At Gandalf's request, he enters the city by night, disguised as a Ranger, and tends to all the wounded, especially Faramir, Éowyn and Merry. He alone is able to heal them by mixing an herb called athelas but nicknamed "king's foil" in water and washing the wounds with it. (The film *The Fellowship of the Ring* hints at this by having Aragorn send Samwise to find king's foil to try to heal Frodo's poisoned wound.)

In addition to being a reference to the legends concerning St. Edward the Confessor, which would have been familiar to Tolkien, these healings further establish Aragorn as a figure of the kingly aspect of Christ. Like Christ, who kept His "messianic secret," Aragorn is trying to hide his true identity until the appointed time of the final battle with Sauron, the Dark Lord. Also like Christ, when Aragorn does heal the wounded, the rumor of it spreads, causing the populace to claim that the king has returned. Indeed, the words of Aragorn to Faramir after he heals him "Walk no more in the shadows, but awake!" sound very similar to those Jesus said to the daughter of Jairus: "Little girl, I say to you, arise" (Mark 5:41), the son of the widow of Nain, "Young man, I say to you, arise" (Luke 7:14) and Lazarus, "Lazarus, come forth!" (John 11:43). 🕊

Note: Quotations from Return of the King are taken from The Lord of the Rings: The Return of the King by J.R.R. Tolkien. New York: Del Rey 2003.

CHARLES III: A PHILOSOPHER-KING FOR OUR TIME

Ryan Hunter

Thoughts on the published Coronation Liturgy of King Charles III and Queen Camilla, "Called to Serve":

Lambeth Palace (the seat and office of the primus of the Anglican Communion, the Most Rev. Archbishop of Canterbury) has published the full Coronation Liturgy prepared for the upcoming 6 May Acclamation, Anointing, Coronation, and Enthronement of TM King Charles III and Queen Camilla at Westminster Abbey. It features brief annotated commentaries by HG The Archbishop of Canterbury, Justin Welby.

In six different dichotomous areas---the traditional and the contemporary, the national and the global, the confessional Christian and the ecumenical, the sacred and the secular, the historical and the future-oriented, and the mystical and the constitutional---the text for the Liturgy offers a magnificent harmony and inner balance in keeping with the best of ancient English coronation liturgical traditions dating to the Liber Regalis recensions and earlier.

The music---including both new compositions and ones reused and adapted from the coronation of HM Queen Elizabeth II in June 1953 and earlier coronations---tends toward the sombre and traditional, in keeping with the King's lifelong aesthetic passion for classical music across the world and in particular in Britain. We can rest assured that the music will not only be magnificent, as all coronation anthems and odes should be, but that the King personally oversaw the selection of the pieces to match with and convey a particular point about the significance of a certain aspect or emphasis in the ceremonies.

Replete with the full majesty of Authorised Version (KJV) biblical psalmody married to new but reverently-wrought supplications to address the multi-confessional, pluralistic realities of twenty-first century Britain, the coronation's theme, "Called to Serve", is unambiguously Christian in origin yet universal, inclusive, supra-confessional, and trans-dogmatic in scope and intentionality. It is in keeping with the core Christian notion of Christ coming to earth as a Servant-King and self-humbling deity, and in keeping with the King's (and his late mother Queen Elizabeth's) oft-stated vision of the British monarchy as a sacred commitment of dedicated, noble service to the British people, and to the global Commonwealth family of nations.

In fidelity to his mother the late Queen's legacy of sacrificial servant-leadership---she beautifully signed what was to become her final testament to her people and the world on her Platinum Jubilee "Your servant, Elizabeth R"---the new King will open his coronation by praying aloud for the first time in recorded history, before the whole world, in humble entreaty to Christ, the King of kings who became the Servant of servants, for divine aid in bearing his sacred trust of service to his peoples. It is as a servant of God, and servant of servants---ancient papal titles adapted by Pope Gregory I, and also for Christ in Christian theology and Muhammad in Islamic theology---that Charles will come humbly before God to be anointed (christos) as a visible sign for his people of God's mercy, justice, and love.

The King will be robed in vestments refitted and altered from the 1953, 1937, and 1911 coronations of his mother, maternal grandfather, and maternal great-grandfather, respectively. The robes' design obviously derives from medieval Catholic episcopal clerical robes. In Catholic, Orthodox, and High Church Anglican understanding, the robes reflect the persistent power of the mediaeval view of the monarch as a profoundly blessed, changed individual from the moment of his anointing---a *mixta persona*, part-layman, part *sacerdote* (priest). At the climax of the service---the anointing, not the physical crowning itself, which comes

after---the King will be anointed by the Archbishop of Canterbury whilst sitting on or kneeling before St Edward's Chair, as numerous of his ancestors were, upon the forehead, hands, and breast with sacred chrism. One of the most extraordinary things about this coronation ceremony is that the chrism for the King and Queen's anointing has been blessed, for the first time ever in recorded history, by the reigning Orthodox Patriarch Theophilos III of Jerusalem. This means that Charles will be the first monarch in England in over five centuries---Henry VIII and his first wife Queen Catherine of Aragon were crowned in 1509 in the last pre-Reformation coronation in England, while Henry's great-niece Mary Queen of Scots was anointed and crowned according to Catholic rites as an infant in 1542 ---to be anointed with blessed chrism which all catholic and orthodox Christians regard as truly blessed and holy according to the principle of Apostolic Succession.

The King clearly sees the chief function or telos of constitutional monarchy today as supra-political and supra-confessional, as an instrument of societal healing, unity, and service, and the purpose of the coronation ceremonies is above all to seek God's blessings, aid, and grace in helping him and his consort carry out their duties to this end. Thus, the wording of the King's successive constitutional oaths---while firmly rooted in British Christian precedent and liturgical tradition---are thus envisioned in Britain's twenty-first century pluralistic ecumenical and interfaith context, extending and embracing beyond the confines of established Church and dogmatic creeds to include all British society.

Ever since the King spent ten weeks as a young man studying Welsh with a Welsh nationalist professor of the Welsh language prior to his 1969 installation as Prince of Wales by his mother, through to his words at his first State Dinner as monarch at Buckingham Palace in which he acknowledged the abuses of power by Britain in South Africa, he has supported efforts to bring about a healing of the harmful aspects of the legacies of English colonialism within (and British colonialism outside) the British Isles. While one cannot predict the future, from the King's many earlier speeches and letters, to his recent openness to public criticism of the failings, abuses, and atrocities of Britain's colonial past---unwelcome to some pro-colonialism reactionaries as they may be---we may hope that he will continue to do as other European monarchs have done in recent years in working and speaking to help heal many of the grievances and traumas of European mercantilist colonialism and maritime slavery. The King's first gestures and statements to this end, in his opening months as monarch, serve a vitally necessary healing role, in fact an aspect of his crucial role as something of secular priest in the body politic of Britannia and the Commonwealth.

The text clearly seeks to keep to the King's vision of fostering (insofar as is possible) universal harmony in society local, regional, national, and global. In an homage to the previously suppressed ethno-linguistic diversity of the four ancient countries of the British Isles, for the first time in known history, several of the supplicatory hymns and responses will be offered in Welsh, Scottish Gaelic, and Irish Gaelic as well as the usual English. For the first time, foreign monarchs have also been invited to attend the coronation, in a gesture of pan-European solidarity in the wake of the ongoing war in Ukraine and drawing attention to twenty-first century Britain's role as one among many in the European and global community of nations.

In a spirit of genuinely inclusive, post-Nostra Aetate-inspired Christian ecumenism, and a nod to Britain's ancient Catholic (and catholic) history, relics including the Gospel of St Augustine of Canterbury will be used, and a Te Deum rendered in Latin, while a solemn Greek prayer of thanksgiving and blessing will serve as an homage to the Greek royal heritage of the King's late father HRH Prince Philip. The Greek linguistic presence in the liturgy (itself a Greek word) also acknowledges the debt which the British coronation rites owe in their earliest antiquity to those of East Rome (Byzantium), which influenced all later European coronation ceremonies from Hungary and Poland to France, the Papacy, and the Holy Roman Empire confederation.

One beautiful innovation---both a nod to contemporary global citizenship and the deliberate involvement of popular participation in the Coronation rites to widen the monarchy's horizontal, participatory touch---is that for the first time in history, those watching around the world will be invited to participate virtually in the acclamation of the King and the loyalty oaths. This novel Homage of the People is thus envisioned as a kind of spiritual communion between king and country and king and Commonwealth (indeed, king and world), welcoming people nationally and globally to join in affirming, blessing, and acclaiming his sacred charges and stewardship duties. This aspect is intended to solidify the emotional bond and contract of understanding between monarch and people in the global internet age, and serves to mirror the King's earlier oaths to govern his peoples according to their respective laws and customs.

Anyone familiar with the King's lifelong Traditionalist philosophical and metaphysical inclinations via Rene Guenon, Martin Lings, Charles Le Gai Eaton, et al. will be pleased to see that the text is a self-consciously, faithful Christian religious service, whose chief purpose throughout---placed as it is within the highest of High Church Anglican Eucharistic liturgies---to serve as an occasional invocation, a calling down, of God's grace upon the new monarch and his consort to aid them in their sacred charge of service to the British people, the peoples of the Commonwealth, and, more broadly, to humanity as a whole. In this sense, the spirit of the text situates it firmly within the Christian confessional milieu, while also being open quite elegantly and naturally to the secular role of the monarch today as a bridge-builder between peoples of faiths and also the increasing number of Britons without religious faith. Thus, we see for the first time the inclusion of leading representatives of Britain's non-Christian faith communities in the ceremonies: the Hindu Prime Minister, in his capacity as UK head of government, will read from the New Testament, while a delegation of Muslim, Jewish, Zoroastrian, Hindu, and Buddhist leaders will present the King with the secular regalia (Christian clergy and peers will present him with those regalia whose origin and symbolism are entirely Christian).

> **Thus, we see for the first time the inclusion of leading representatives of Britain's non-Christian faith communities in the ceremonies**

While current, post-1688 statutory law obliges the King---an avowed Traditionalist-Perennialist who once remarked that he wished to serve as either Defender of Faith (as such, in a predominatingly secular age) or Faiths (in a pluralistic Britain) rather than as the post-Henrican Defender of the (Anglican) Faith---to publicly avow himself to be "a faithful Protestant" and pledge to defend the established Anglican Protestant religion "according to law", the controversial anti-Catholic confessional nature of this pledge has been deliberately and necessarily softened in this ecumenical and increasingly secular age. Introductory attestations, to be made by the Archbishop of Canterbury as Primus of the Church of England, will proclaim that the self-conscious role of the established Church today---according to its own latest social, ecumenical, and interfaith vision---is to work, non-dogmatically, toward a pluralistic society in which all faiths may flourish freely in Britain. This postmodern inclusivity, in which the Church of England has surrendered any claim to possess The Truth as such in any exclusivist sense, is in deliberate contrast to the earlier predominating Anglican view of the Church itself (at least before the so-called Glorious Revolution) as constituting the only legitimate Church in England and Ireland. The Church of England has thus arrived at a point utterly removed from its first nearly two centuries, when it regularly sought royal intervention and state power, even inviting the overthrow of the anointed and crowned King James VII and II in 1688, to maintain its established position and impose its particular doctrines on other churches and peoples (especially recusant Roman Catholics and low church Protestant Nonconformists) following the Henrican, Edwardian, and Elizabethan Reformations.

A lifelong supporter of interfaith dialogue and respect, the King has made several pilgrimages to the Orthodox monastic centre of Mount Athos, of whose benevolent society he long served as chief Patron. As Prince of Wales, he endowed numerous interfaith-oriented traditional educational programs and scholarly efforts such as The Prince's Trust, Temenos Academy, and The Prince's School for Traditional Arts. His inaugural speech in the 1990s opening the Oxford Centre for Islamic Studies gratified Muslims in Britain and across the world with his deep knowledge and evident appreciation for the many contributions of Islamic civilisation to the world's heritage. Since his accession in September, the King has publicly attended a London Sikh gurdwara, a Jewish synagogue, a Ukrainian Catholic cathedral, and many Anglican churches.

One of the clearest examples of the continuation of holy tradition in the ceremony is that its most sacred moment---the solemn anointing of the monarch upon the forehead, hands, and breast in the kingly-prophetic style of Solomon---will take place behind a specially-built panelled screen, so that it will be for the King the only private moment of the entire ceremony in which he is hidden from the cameras and the view of the congregation, and thus alone with God. In elegant contrast, to demonstrate that a queen consort's authority and status flows from the crown---and thus from her husband as monarch---Queen Camilla will be anointed only upon the forehead, and in public view, but with the same chrism used to effect the anointing of her husband. Keeping with the anointing and coronation of Queen Elizabeth in 1937, Queen Mary in 1911, and Queen Alexandra in 1902 shortly following that of their husband-kings, this subtle difference in the anointing between monarch-husband and consort-wife perfectly symbolises that the queen consort shares naturally in her husband's dignity, style, and rank, but that her authority deries from her marriage to him, while his authority as monarch derives (as the ceremony daringly insists in a republican age with few remaining ancient monarchies)

directly from God, practically manifested and maintained in ordinary time by Parliamentary and popular accord.

The coronation will thus be visibly in accord with ancient English and other Christian mediaeval notions of the sacred ceremony serving as an 'eighth sacrament' (in Catholic tradition, or ordinance in Protestant tradition), and in this 'post-modern' age, it will serve as a magnificent, embodied realisation in time and place of the King's philosophical Traditionalism married to the most praiseworthy and laudable aspects of modern British society today. The text---a tantalising foretaste of what we can as of now only imagine and conceptualise before the Coronation itself on Saturday, 6 May---elegantly balances the best of early English mediaeval coronation precedent, recognition of the unique linguistic heritage of the four countries comprising the British Isles, and the diverse religious pluralism and multi-ethnic composition of Britain today.

The coronation of a new monarch serves as a mirror by which a society sees itself reflected in the person assuming the sacred mantle of authority and trust over and as the keystone and formal fountain-head of the body politic. The supra-political monarch serves as a looking-glass, a calm and steady mirror in which an ever-changing people may see in themselves their best, highest, and noblest aspirations. King Charles' coronation---as the first in seven decades---thus proclaims and publicises both how British society has progressed and changed over his lifetime, and what it has stalwartly preserved, conserved, and maintained in its national character and psyche. The seven decades of his mother's unprecedented reign witnessed the end of global empires and the UK's evolution from global (if declining) post-war empire to present-day composite, mid-sized union of four nations-in-one state. As the longest-serving heir to any throne, as a man steeped in the lifelong study of history, philosophy, and the arts along with statesmanship and government, King Charles III stands uniquely as the best-studied and best-prepared monarch in British history. He is a living icon (image) and bridge recalling the stoic dedication and self-sacrifice of his parents' Second World War generation, and the optimism, friendliness, and accessibility of his son and heir and his heirs beyond. He stands not only between colonial empire and post-colonial state, but between the resolutely Protestant Christian Britain of 1953 and the definitely multi-faith and secular Britain of 2023.

The coronation solemnising the new reign thus spans the conceptual divide between parliamentary constitutional government and sacred divine right, between modernity and antiquity, new and old, and projects Britain's self-concept of its role in a more egalitarian, post-colonial, interconnected world. It projects a monarchy confident in having long foresworn the 'efficient' aspects of coercive political statecraft and factional partisanship to have in its place carved for itself a far more

powerful, transcendent, stable, and dignified role. As the paramount civil institution in British society, the monarchy alone may serve as a unifying focal point for healing historical memory outside of and beyond ephemeral partisan political considerations. It alone may serve, in contrast to the ever-changing push and pull of parliamentary partisan politics, as a stable guide and reference between past, present, and future, and a sure ballast of service, duty, and evolving tradition in the stormy seas of uncharted postmodernity.

Looking thus to both the noblest aspects of over a millennium of Britain's pre-colonial Christian past and its post-colonial, pluralistic future, the coronation of the new king and his queen will splendidly solemnise the third Carolinean age to the nation and the world as Britons seek God's blessings for their new servant-leader. May Britons of all beliefs, backgrounds, and becomings unite, and peoples of goodwill across the Anglosphere and Commonwealth share, in prayerful devotion, singing as one body the old anthem, in truth a prayer adapted from the Psalmist Prophet-King David: God Save the King.

SAINT CASIMIR

The Traveling Troubadour

One such exemplary figure of spiritual fortitude was Prince Casimir of Poland, who would later become the country's beloved patron saint. Living in the 15th century, he was a highly educated and intellectual young man, yet most importantly, he embraced true humility and strove for justice and fairness towards his people. He embodied grace-filled sanctity, and was a beacon of pious clarity and conviction, reflecting the graces of God's eternal light by choosing to bow to the heavenly throne over the throne of man.

Since he came from a long lineage of royalty, with his dutiful father, Casimir IV, ruling as King of Poland, and his loving mother Elisabeth as his Queen, he was expected someday to follow in their footsteps and wear the crown. Although he had a great interest in brokering peace between countries through diplomacy, he had little desire to attain victories on the battlefield. As a young prince, Casimir became head of the realm for several years out of obedience to father who had to leave the country to attend to his responsibilities as Grand Duke of Lithuania. Casimir ruled with a compassionate and conscientious and justice that was greatly admired in the eyes of those citizens under his dominion.

This scourge of consumption, also known as tuberculosis, was dreaded as "the white plague" due to the paleness of the skin of those who contracted it. Those stricken had to fight for every breath, and their condition deteriorated at a rapid, and progressively painful, pace. Casimir tragically contracted this agonizing affliction. During the Middle Ages, it was believed that God gave the power of healing touch to the true line of royalty, but it wasn't his fate to receive it himself. One wonders if he perhaps caught the fatal disease from carrying out that very custom on behalf of those among his flock who were helplessly and hopelessly inflicted. Even when he was wracked in agony, he endured the suffering with an gracious acceptance of the Almighty's will and continued his sacrificial obligations as an instrument of love. At last, his life ebbed away on March 4, 1484. He was only 23 years of age.

Through Casimir, providence presented the world with a briefly flickering candle, shining the light of

Artwork: *Saint Casimir Giving Alms* by Kazimierz Mirecki, 1884 true selfless love through his virtuous life and long-suffering faithfulness. Yet the eternal flame of his resilient devotion will never be extinguished. After five hundred years, his example of piety remains hallowed in the hearts of the Polish people as a brilliant beacon of spiritual hopefulness in a world of strife and darkness. His tomb became a shrine famous for many miracles, and he was canonized in 1522. He is also the patron of the Knights of St. John and is invoked against the enemies of the faith and Poland. When his mortal remains were exhumed to be moved to a chapel being built in his honor 120 years after his death, they were found by the Vatican's ecclesiastical authorities to be intact and incorrupt.

A parchment of his favorite devotional hymn, "Omni die dic Mariae", was also discovered within the casket. Thereafter it became widely known as "The Prayer of Saint Casimir."

The essence and focus of Casimir's loyalty was centered on the steadfast commitment of serving Christ's Kingdom above the kingdoms of men. This author was born into the "Faith of Our Fathers", with Catholic ancestry on both his paternal and maternal sides, including a quarter slice of Polish heritage. He was christened on Sunday March 4 at The Church of the Madonna. As providence would have it, this was the Feast Day of Saint Casimir, the Pious Polish Prince.

Coats of arms of Poland
by unknown artist, 19th century

CREDITS

Chessboard model:	Kilt2007
End-piece illustrations: (pp. 11, 15, 19, 24, 27, 39, 42, 49, 51, 55, 63, 67, 71, 77, 94, 101, 109, 113, 115, 118, 126, 131, 137, 149, 152)	Generated by Midjourney.
(p. 83)	Public domain.
Artwork and photos (pp. 3, 6, 7, 12, 16, 20, 28, 40, 43, 44, 56, 58, 60, 68, 78, 88, 95, 96, 98, 102, 106, 110, 116, 120, 127, 128, 132, 138, 150, 152):	As cited (public domain).
Editor-in-Chief:	Avellina Balestri
Editorial and Graphic Design:	Mark Anderson
Proofreaders/Editors:	Avellina Balestri Guy Jackson Jason Plessas Gabriel Connor Salter Jo Sexton

NEXT ISSUE

Our Next Issue... *The Founding of America*

Fellowship & Fairydust is looking for articles, stories, poems, and artwork pertaining to early American history, from the founding of the colonies by European powers through to the American Revolution and the early years of the new republic of the United States of America.

DISCLAIMER

WEBSITE

https://fellowshipandfairydust.com/

Fellowship & Fairydust

2023

Printed in Great Britain
by Amazon

22838248R10090